A GOOD TIME FOR THE TRUTH

A GOOD TIME FOR THE TRUTH

RACE IN MINNESOTA

EDITED BY SUN YUNG SHIN

MINNESOTA
HISTORICAL
SOCIETY PRESS

The publication of this book was supported through a generous grant from the June D. Holmquist Publications and Research Fund.

www.mnhspress.org

The Minnesota Historical Society Press is a member of the Association of American University Presses.

Manufactured in the United States of America

10 9 8

∞ The paper used in this publication meets the minimum requirements of the American National Standard for Information Sciences—Permanence for Printed Library Materials, ANSI Z39.48-1984.

International Standard Book Number
ISBN: 978-1-68134-002-9 (paper)
ISBN: 978-1-68134-003-6 (e-book)

Library of Congress Cataloging-in-Publication Data
Names: Shin, Sun Yung, editor.
Title: A good time for the truth : race in Minnesota / edited by Sun Yung Shin.
Description: St. Paul, MN : Minnesota Historical Society Press, 2016. |
    Includes bibliographical references.
Identifiers: LCCN 2015045307 | ISBN 9781681340029 (pbk. : alk. paper) |
    ISBN 9781681340036 (ebook)
Subjects: LCSH: Minnesota—Race relations.
Classification: LCC F615.A1 G66 2016 | DDC 305.8009776—dc23
LC record available at http://lccn.loc.gov/2015045307

This and other Minnesota Historical Society Press books are available from popular e-book vendors.

CONTENTS

A GOOD TIME FOR THE TRUTH

INTRODUCTION

Sun Yung Shin

You hold in your hand a book of visions. Memories. True stories. Shock. Grief. Dreams. Activism. Recognition. A call for us to listen and learn about one another's real lives in Minnesota.

It is time for this book. It is always a good time for the truth, for those who have often been spoken for and about to speak for themselves. The voices in this anthology provide a forum: a multifaceted, dazzling view of life in the state beyond the stereotypes, under *Minnesota Nice*, and into the possibilities for our future.

People of color are the fastest growing segment of Minnesota's population. But is Minnesota a state that understands "race"? What does it mean to be "raced"? Although race is not a biological or genetic reality, it nonetheless continues to be very real in terms of its influence on the lives of Indigenous people and people of color. What are those effects, and what do they mean for people's lives?

This anthology begins to answer those questions, but it is not meant to address every aspect of race and culture in the state. Nor are the contributors meant, as a group, to represent or speak for every ethnicity and racial group in Minnesota. Not only would that be nearly impossible, it is not desirable. This is merely a small, but powerful, selection. As the first book of its kind in Minnesota, it is one wave in a larger movement toward equality. It is here that those in the minority stand in the majority, under the spotlight. Their stories are front and center. Please consider them on their own terms, and know that each author is but one individual. One essay by one Minnesotan connecting with another Minnesotan at a time, book in hand, words on the page.

These contributors may, however, speak with the collective,

intergenerational wisdom (and grief, and loss, and strength, and joy) of one or more communities. All of us alive today are the product of our ancestors' survival and regeneration. When we work for freedom, we stand on the shoulders, sacrifices, activism, reflection, self-knowledge, and persistence of those who come before us.

These writers have stepped forward and have been included here because they are established or emerging creative writers who have long been committed to writing and working creatively on issues of race, culture, and social justice. Struggling together toward a fair and vibrant civil society in Minnesota—a goal which must include the naming of and dismantling of racism. The writers are also activists and educators, and they fulfill many other roles in their/our communities. This is a book of stories, not of policy recommendations or ideologies, though at least one contributor has a master's degree in public policy. This is not a book of theory or of research, though many have advanced degrees and several are professors. While these pieces are crafted with fine literary skill, it could be argued that this anthology is more in the spirit and lineage of oral tradition, of handing down knowledge and values through stories.

I love a good anthology because it can be like a circle—everyone is equal. Yes, there is an order from front to back, but it need not be read in that order. It is completely up to the reader, and no single voice carries more weight than another. This is a radical equality. Some of the contributors are well known nationally, and others are beginning their writing careers. No matter—you will find yourself entering the world of each essay fully, alive to the unique sensitivities, curiosity, emotions, and intelligence of its author.

―――――――

It is hard to talk about race across racial lines. Race is ingrained in societal systems and institutions, conferring a system of advantages upon members of the dominant group. This means that people's realities, their *lived experiences*, differ. Race is often invisible to those who benefit, willingly or unwillingly, knowingly or unknowingly. It is entirely visible to those who do not benefit.

No one wants to make an observation or share an injury regarding their race and have it be dismissed, misunderstood, mocked, or worse. No one wants to feel that they are participating, even passively, in the oppression or harm of others. No one wants to believe that inequality persists and limits children's futures and abilities to fulfill their potential.

There are some hard truths, though, that we must understand and agree upon. Race was invented by white people, Europeans colonizing the globe, as a pseudoscientific justification for the subjugation of people of color. Race theory and racecraft were often paired with Christianization missions to subdue, convert, assimilate, or simply destroy Indigenous people, who were figured as heathens who needed saving and who were not worthy of the bountiful natural resources of the "New World," of Africa, of Asia. Historians of race have researched, documented, and eloquently described this history. As too is the atrocity that was the mid-Atlantic slave trade and the vicious institution of chattel slavery as practiced in the American South. As too is the resulting legal abolition of slavery but the evolution of peonage and other systems that kept African Americans in bondage long after Emancipation and the end of the Civil War.

There is a tremendous amount of scholarship, activism, education, and community work being done across the country and in Minnesota to help us recognize and dismantle racism. Because understanding race and racism is not merely about mapping the contours of the lives of people of color, this work also involves understanding whiteness and the maintenance of often invisible systems of white privilege. A great place to start learning that history is *The History of White People* by Dr. Nell Irvin Painter. White American scholars Robin DiAngelo, Joe Feagin, and many others are doing fascinating work on what they are calling "white fragility" and "white racial frames," respectively.

This book, though, offers different insights. Most people of color in the United States have to think about race every day, multiple times a day. We are constantly negotiating our bodies and our selves, our identities, in a racialized society. How we look, and who our people are or are assumed to be, are relentlessly measured against a white ideal and mostly found inferior. We are nearly invisible—or painted negatively as criminals, victims, charity cases without history or agency—in the news, arts, literature, curricula, political platforms. We are the butts of jokes. We are racially profiled. We fear a backlash when anyone who looks like us or could be mistaken for us commits an infraction or crime. We know others may question our legitimacy to be in a specific space or job—or even to be in this country. We experience professional isolation. Those of us who are in the middle class or hold white-collar jobs are usually one of the few—or the only—people of color in the room, in the institution.

We also know there are many white people who work and have worked in solidarity with us. There are white people who see their liberation as tied to ours.

———

As residents of a state and territory that is wealthy in resources (Indigenous knowledge shared with early European traders; abundant waterways, forests, minerals, soil; hardworking immigrants in every generation) and has been an economic and quality-of-life success story in so many ways, Minnesotans cannot continue to bury the lede in the national conversation about us. Some progress has been made in Minnesota toward eliminating racial disparities, but things have gotten worse in some notable ways, including racial diversity among K-12 teachers, poverty rates for children of color, access to fresh food and exercise and play, declining real wages, and job security for the parents and caregivers of those children. The children of color growing up in Minnesota today are subject to those limiting beliefs, often unacknowledged and unbidden, held by those in charge of their education, health care, and physical safety in public and private spaces. Shortages of school counselors, teachers, mental health care providers, and so on impact most those with the least. People are advocating and mobilizing for their rights and for the rights of "common" people (not the owning class, the 1 percent) every day. People resist, build capacity personally and organizationally, and effect change.

One bedrock principle of a democracy is that there should be safeguards against tyranny of the majority. What is just and fair for the whole society must be enacted and upheld, not what always benefits the majority just because of numbers. Because minority groups everywhere are vulnerable, the U.S. Constitution guarantees the rights of the minority. Racism has been a tyrant in America and there is no excuse for its continued existence. To banish this tyrant, we need understanding. We need to peel back any convenient myths and stereotypes and be real with one another. In her now-famous and oft-quoted TED talk, "The Danger of a Single Story," Nigerian American novelist Chimamanda Ngozi Adichie said, "The problem with stereotypes is not that they are untrue, but that they are incomplete. They make one story become the only story." None of us should have one story of what it means and is to be Indigenous, Black, Vietnamese, Guatemalan, Iranian, and so on. Whether in Minnesota or elsewhere. The footprint of the United States is too vast for any of us to set aside this responsibility and opportunity.

———————

A society that systematically suppresses the stories and wisdom of certain groups cannot make the best decisions for a shared future. We need a future in this state that leaves no one out. We are interconnected, we are interdependent. In the long run, on our earth, we will thrive or fail together. Those of us who have not always had places at the table, so to speak, want to be heard and understood. Naturally, we all want to have a say in what happens to us and around us. This value, this commitment to free speech, is, of course, in the Bill of Rights, and it is a requirement for the flourishing and maintenance of any true democratic society.

In the transracial and transnational adoption community, some of us have adopted a motto, "Nothing about us without us," *Nihil de nobis, sine nobis,* which was used widely in the United

States, first by disability activists in the 1990s, and in Central Europe before that. In the introduction to an anthology I co-edited with Jane Jeong Trenka and Chinyere Oparah, *Outsiders Within: Writing on Transracial Adoption*, we explained that we transracial and transnational adoptees have long been subject to research that has objectified us and obscured our adult perspectives. Policies and laws, and media reportage, continue to proliferate without our input, although, through persistent and strategic activism, we are changing the dynamic. We are speaking for ourselves, are representing ourselves in media and in courts of law, and are no longer silent, invisible except as objects of study or as children complicit in kinship and child welfare discourse that silences us as adult agents. Despite conflicts, setbacks, and ongoing struggles, I have seen great progress and change, from margin to center. Like many of us, I believe in stories and in the bone-deep knowledge of those inside a certain experience, whether that is race, gender, dis/ability, family system, and so on.

Of course, the struggle for justice never ends. We will not dismantle racism and then be "done." Power will always seek to justify, defend, and maintain itself, in all its manifestations. That is the struggle for survival. Adapt, or perish, whether as an individual or as a group. We are facing this challenge on our planet today. As we seek justice—and survival of our, and many other, species—we must acknowledge the importance of our identities, which often flow from the positions into which we are born and the positions into which we are placed by the powers that be.

Our identities are also made out of our innate material. Our genes, our physical inheritances, our intergenerational embodied memories. Our identities in society are intersectional—profoundly overlapping and complicated. This is not a new concept, and it is one that must always be addressed when we are parsing out threads of meaning and powerful constructs such as "race" and the realities that racialized policies and relationships engender and maintain. None of us is just one thing, and each axis is dynamic and interacts with the others. No one is "white" and also not, for example, a woman, or a member of the

LGBTQ or gender-nonconforming community, or poor, or rich, or disabled, or Muslim, or Buddhist, or atheist, or a member of any other in/voluntary category that may carry with it advantages and disadvantages.

Race is certainly not always the most important dimension of our identities, but in Minnesota, and in the United States, it is undeniably important. Too often, in a split second, it can become a life-or-death matter. It can determine much of our destinies, our movements, our opportunities, our vulnerabilities. It has determined who has been taken from their families and sent to assimilationist and abusive boarding schools, who has been allowed to work and for how long, who has been allowed to live in certain neighborhoods, who is stopped and frisked, who has access to financing and opportunity and good education and safety. The structures built in the past live with us, just as systems we build now will exist after us.

So what does racial "progress" look like? An elimination of differences? Certainly not. We will have to co-create the future. A future not of "tolerance" but of a kind of pluralism that thrives because of fairness, a fairness that comes from a truth and reconciliation process that leaves no people's stories untold. This may or may not be progress, depending on where you stand. I've been reminded many times that Indigenous people and nations do not as a whole want "social progress," do not want new laws and new policies. They want broken treaties to be revisited and finally upheld. They want stolen lands and resources returned. They want their legal sovereignty and rights upheld, as do all nations and peoples. Indigenous peoples have and can and do speak for themselves, so I will stop there, but it is a good reminder that there is radical diversity within the world of people who are "non-white."

But that term—"non-white"—is offensive language to many. "Non-white" both ignores the radical diversity among people and defines people in the negative. Interracial and interethnic conflict and enmity among "non-whites" can and does exist in U.S. communities and in countries and regions beyond the borders of the United States. And it must be said that the term "people of color," which I am using in this introduction for consistency, is a politicized category, not all purpose, not embraced by all, useful in some contexts but not in others, and will no doubt eventually be replaced entirely by one or more new terms.

Language is charged. Language is self-representation. Language is one of the sets of DNA of a culture. (While all of the essays in this anthology are in English, I want us to keep in mind that the United States has no official language. This is significant, an opening, a kind of flexibility.) What we call each other can show respect or disrespect. In this introduction I have chosen to use "Indigenous" rather than a variety of other terms that can depend on context because that is what the contributors used in their essays. Contributors have decided for themselves about the capitalization of B/black and W/white.

―――――

Culture is human nature. We created the culture of racism and we can unmake it, we can transform old ways into new and better ways. We can recall old ways that worked well and bring them into the present. We have choices. As the centenarian civil rights activist Grace Lee Boggs liked to say, everything changes and we can't get stuck in old ideas. Racism is an old idea. A tradition that harms children is not worth conserving or continuing. Life is wealth and relationships are wealth. Domination, subjugation, exploitation, and the luxury of looking away is a poverty of the soul. But we have choices. We can learn and grow.

Racism continues to divide us as a nation as we have too often failed, collectively, to address the issues of the past and to seek truth in the present. Many readers may notice that Americans are having more, and more urgent, conversations—and many highly visible public demonstrations—about race in this country, as there is a renewed critical mass of citizens and groups and leaders who are unafraid to speak the truth about these disparities and about the very real suffering of and harsh punishments meted out to certain communities and groups.

These essays are offered as contributions to that conversation. They are intended to enlarge our understanding of, and deepen our connections to, one another. These writers are here to feed our spirits, if we let them. As readers and listeners we have an important job to do, a powerful and empowering attitude to assume: "Tell me the truth of the matter. When I don't understand, I will not protest or judge or correct, I will simply listen harder. I am here to recognize you as my fellow human being with a story."

The contributors have given us a splendid gift, the gift of touching another human being's inner reality, behind masks and veils and politeness. They are bringing us generously into their experiences, experiences that shape Minnesota, experiences that we must understand if we are to come together in real relationships across sometimes very difficult borders. We can read their stories and leave each one with a deeper, more complex understanding of how race and culture are lived in Minnesota—and better prepared for the conversations and changes ahead.

The tragic story of American racism has continued to unfold in Minnesota and across the country as we put the final touches on this book. We cannot list all the names of all the people of color and Indigenous people, in our community and elsewhere, who have suffered and died because of the violent, hate-filled, or grossly negligent actions of individuals whose culpability is being evaluated as I write—and no doubt as you read. Good people of all backgrounds want those individuals to be brought to justice. We want our society to be utterly transformed.

Activists and artists and cultural and community workers and people of conscience continue to organize, struggle, and sacrifice in order to right the historical wrongs in our society. Racism, like any deeply embedded system of privilege, won't be dismantled in one fell swoop. But good people need to take action continuously, and I would say daily, until it is dismantled. Because lives are at stake, every day: on sidewalks, in doctor's offices, in the waiting room of the bank, and most importantly, in classrooms.

I believe we can do it. I know I am not alone in this conviction.

People of color and Indigenous people know with a specific, agonizing intimacy that racism was constructed and upheld by white society (in spaces such as the police precinct, the courtroom, school board meetings, newsrooms, Hollywood studios, mortgage loan offices, and everywhere power has resided in America) in order to confer unearned advantages on white people. It's really as simple as that. It's not a law of nature. It's culture. It's something we made, invented, maintained. Since it was made, like a vast machine, it can be unmade, and it must. We—that is to say, good people—are not asking that every bias and prejudice be rooted out and destroyed or transformed; we are not the thought police. We want truth to see the light of day; we want a fair system.

Niceness is not fairness.

Peace (or the absence of open conflict) is not justice.

Comfort is not guaranteed.

Until we dismantle this system, we will insist, in words and actions: Change is necessary. We offer this book to speed that change.

◆ FEAR OF A BLACK MOTHER

Shannon Gibney

Shannon Gibney is a writer, educator, activist, and the author of
See No Color, a young adult novel. Her writing has appeared in
Al Jazeera America, The Crisis, Gawker, and other venues. A Bush
Artist and McKnight Writing Fellow, she lives with her husband and
children in Minneapolis.

My family and I stroll into the co-op on a Saturday night, looking for some fresh fruit, milk, and meat. The grocery is a seven-
minute drive from our house, and its patrons reflect the solidly
middle-class, hippie character of the neighborhood right next to
ours. The co-op skews a bit whiter than the South Minneapolis
communities it is part of, mostly because so many people of color
are priced out by its high-quality, organic products.

"Over there," I say, pointing to a large bushel of peaches to the
right of the entrance.

My husband and I start heading toward the succulent fruits,
but our two-and-a-half-year-old son, inspired by his ongoing
quest for refined sugar, heads in the exact opposite direction.
On the other side of the checkout lines sits a quiet, fastidiously
organized, delicious paradise of pie and cake slices of every variety, made only from the finest ingredients, individually packed
in plastic containers. My son knows this because on the way out
of the store, my husband and I often can't resist admiring the
delicate confections and, on occasion, buying one for dessert. As
instant gratification is the modus operandi of toddler mind, however, my son has decided that there is really no point in waiting
for this step of the trip to arrive.

"Babe," I say to Ballah, pointing at our son. "Please get him."

My husband nods his assent and takes off in pursuit of Boisey.

I turn my attention to the task at hand and, before long, am completely immersed in selecting the juiciest, freshest peaches. I am drawn to the corn on the cob case, and I pick up a two-gallon container of milk, and then I realize that it would be prudent to find my husband and son. Ballah, a Liberian immigrant, has been in-country for less than two years at this point, and he is still very much in the middle of learning the intricate minutiae and subtle cultural cues of contemporary American culture. He is sometimes misinterpreted, or he misinterprets someone else or a situation, so I like to keep tabs on him—especially around white people. Our experience so far has been that most white people see him as a young, uneducated, dark-skinned African immigrant man, and they sometimes feel emboldened to act on this view, talking to him in ways they would *never* talk to me: a light-skinned, highly educated Black American professional woman. It shocked both of us the first time it happened, but now we are both used to it, and have adapted. I think what galls them even more is seeing a Black father actively engaged with his son; it creates a kind of cognitive dissonance with the mainstream images of "The Absent/Misogynist Black Father" they have eagerly imbibed from the mainstream media, but which they can't possibly articulate, for fear of exposing their white liberal minds to the reality of their deep-seated racism. If living in Minnesota has taught me one thing, it is that people will lash out at whoever tries to show what sits behind the appearance of things, especially if their own bias is the culprit.

Just beyond the aisles of 100-percent-whole-wheat flours, fair-trade chocolates, and recycled paper products, the Sacred Wall of Delectable Treats appears, and I see Boisey holding something in his hand. Beside him, a young white male employee appears to be lecturing him sternly. My stomach churns, and I look for Ballah, but he is nowhere to be seen.

As I approach the two of them, I reach out and affectionately rub Boisey's head of raucous curls. "What's going on?" I ask, my eyes moving from my son's to the man's.

Boisey scrunches his face into a half grin, and I see that he is holding a package of chocolate banana pie in his hand, that it has been opened, and that there is a telltale lump of it on his right index finger.

"Oh," I say, catching on.

The employee crosses his arms in front of his chest.

I crouch down, so that I am at my son's level. "Did you open this?"

Boisey's face goes from mischievous to guilty in about one second flat. Still, he shakes his head.

I sigh. "Did you open this, and then eat some?"

Boisey looks like he is trying to find a way out of this, a way away from me, but now I'm tightly holding his free hand.

"Remember, we don't lie," I say. "Lying makes people not trust us."

Boisey's eyes slowly make their way back to mine, and he nods slowly, remorse finally starting to seep in.

"Thank you for telling me the truth," I tell my son. "But I need you to remember next time that we don't touch things that aren't ours."

Boisey nods slowly again, and I can see we are maybe twenty seconds away from a full-on cry. Not necessarily because he lied or ate the pie, but because he has disappointed his mommy.

I squeeze his hand and stand up. "I'm so sorry about this, sir," I say to the employee, still standing there, still observing the scene. I don't get the sense that he is actually *angry* with my son or about what he has done, but he is definitely not pleased. "We'll pay for this, of course," I tell him, gesturing toward the pie piece, now sliding sideways in its plastic container, as my son's other hand drops. Warm tears fall on both of our hands.

The man nods, then says, "He also opened this one, and was about to take a bite out of it, too," he says, picking up another piece of pie, this one strawberry.

Boisey's face collapses under this new revelation, and he begins to wail.

The man is staring at me intensely, I realize. Implicit in his gaze is a critique of my parenting, the statement, *You should do a better job of taking care of your child*. Of course, this is hardly the first time I have dealt with this sentiment—whether stated on unstated. Our culture is as judgmental and overly critical of mothers as any other, and almost all of my friends who are mothers, regardless of their race or cultural background, have dealt with this in some way. There is, however, a very particular flavor of disdain for the Black mother that I have picked up on through my experiences— one quite distinct from that of the Asian American, Latina, Native, or white mother. It is more like a confirmation than a slow discovery. *Oh. I knew you didn't know what you were doing. These children are always unruly anyway, and the mothers just don't care.* That is what I am picking up on from this young white man in front of me. And I am entirely sure that he has no idea that this is what he deeply believes, or that this is the energy he is casting on to me, and my son. I struggle to not turn to anger, which I know will only inflame the situation. *Where is Ballah?* That is the other question bubbling up in the back of my mind.

"My sincere apologies," I say, resorting to the middle-class etiquette that my parents taught me so well. "Of course, we'll pay for everything and will make sure this won't happen again. Sorry for the inconvenience."

Boisey is halfway to hollering now, his small face buried in the folds of my skirt. His daily struggle is that he is not only two and a half, and therefore battling all the normal impulses that come with the age, but also extremely sensitive, just like his mother. Now, finally understanding that what he did was "bad," he is almost inconsolable.

The employee nods, apparently placated by my answer, if not satisfied by it. I say a silent prayer for class codes, which can sometimes get you out of sticky situations when race is a liability.

As the man turns and walks away, Ballah casually comes up. "What happened?" he asks, nodding toward Boisey.

"Never mind," I say, dragging all of us toward the checkout line. People are beginning to look, as the volume of Boisey's crying is turned up. "I'll tell you once we get out of here."

I've been wonderin' why
People livin' in fear
Of my shade
(Or my hi top fade)
I'm not the one that's runnin'
But they got me on the run
Treat me like I have a gun
All I got is genes and chromosomes
Consider me Black to the bone
All I want is peace and love
On this planet
(Ain't that how God planned it?)

Excuse us for the news
You might not be amused
But did you know White comes from Black?
No need to be confused

Excuse us for the news
I question those accused
Why is this fear of Black from White
Influence who you choose?

—Public Enemy, "Fear of a Black Planet"

I soon gathered that being perceived as dangerous is a hazard
in itself. I only needed to turn a corner into a dicey situation,
or crowd some frightened, armed person in a foyer some-
where, or make an errant move after being pulled over by a
policeman. Where fear and weapons meet—and they often do
in urban America—there is always the possibility of death.

—Brent Staples, "Just Walk On By"[1]

---

[1] Brent Staples, "Just Walk on By: A Black Man Ponders His Ability to Alter Public Space," *Ms. Magazine* (September 1986).

The Black male body is seen as inherently threatening, *just by virtue of its very existence*, both in public spaces as well as in the public imagination. This has been proven and explored in great detail by now, anecdotally and quantitatively, in many forums, and it is not the topic of this essay. The implications of what this writ large menacing of the body means for the mothers of Black children—and Black male children in particular—have received far less attention, however.

Trayvon Martin.
Jordan Davis.
Michael Brown.
Eric Garner.
Tamir Rice.
Eric Harris.
Walter Scott.
Freddie Gray.
And who else, by the time you read this?

These are not just the names of the dead for the Black mother, but possible antecedents to our own son's name in a nightmarish list of young Black male bodies that were seen as both dangerous and completely expendable in the eyes of their executors and in the majority of America. They are eulogy, but also predictable prologue to a mother's worst fears: the death of her child.

And though we may wish for our children to remain children for as long as possible, what we wish more is for them to live, and to grow and flourish into adulthood and on into old age. This requires a delicate balance between educating our sons about the ways they are seen by law enforcement and the general public at increasingly younger ages, before it may be developmentally appropriate, and helping them envelop themselves in the magical world of childhood for as long as possible. My child is six and a half now, thoroughly engrossed in Rescue Bots and Ninjago and bugs, but I am already getting twitchy about the upcoming talks that loom large, talks about holding himself in the classroom, engaging with his teachers and peers, and, most of all, making sure he is giving no one, especially white people, any extra reason to view him *as a Problem or Threat*. As a mother, I know it is my duty to protect him. As a Black citizen in a country that has *never* viewed Black bodies as worthy of protection, I know I cannot.

This is the Fear of the Black Mother.

How do you protect the thing you love most in the world, when it is also the very thing that the world most fears? How do you tell yourself that you can still be there for your child, that you can still be the mother you always wanted to be, when your fears, validated every day by the news of another death of another young Black male child, tell you otherwise?

And this fear is not new. It has been with Black mothers always. Black life has always been conditional in this country, and very well may always be so. Only the specific circumstances of our children's subjugation is new: the stop-and-frisk laws, the drug war and its attendant shocking incarceration rates for working-class young Black and Latino men, the everyday racial profiling through every neighborhood in our city. You get used to it, but you will never get used to it, not for your children. You ask yourself: is that what parenting is? Preparing your child to live in and accept a world in which they are seen as animals? And there is no answer.

When the verdict came down about the Trayvon Martin case, that the jury had found his shooter George Zimmerman not guilty, I couldn't stop crying. I was pregnant with my second child, with just two months until it would arrive in the world, and I was suddenly, shockingly frightened that it would be a boy. Of course, I knew about the history and experiences of Black men in this country before having my son, but never had I felt my own impotence at the thought of keeping him, or another even more fragile being, safe from all the violence that would inevitably come his way, via education, police, employment, health care, housing—essentially, everything that matters in life. Even more depressing was the knowledge that our family's upper-middle-class status would not be able to effectively buffer all of this bias, as evidenced by multiple studies I had read. I holed myself away, distraught and not really feeling fit for public life for days, until I felt I could somehow summon the energy to engage with the outside world in a more productive way. When the baby came, it was a girl. This would have been a relief, except that she was still-born. Apparently, she had changed her mind halfway here and decided that this world, in its current incarnation, was not where she wanted to be.

———

Once we are back from the co-op, I try to explain to Ballah why our son's opening and eating of the pie pieces is perceived as so much more than that. "On some level, mostly unconscious per-haps, they *expect* him to take something," I say.

"Because he is a Black boy," Ballah says slowly, letting the full import of the words sink in.

"Yes," I say. "Because he is a Black boy, and for no other reason."

My husband frowns, disbelieving, perhaps, in the prevalence of these kinds of insidious social biases in this New Land of Op-portunity that he and so many new immigrants are striving to make their home. Still, he has been pulled over by police three times already this summer, about three minutes from our house, while driving to the gym. Each time, the officer runs his license in the system, and when nothing comes up, insists that he pulled him over because it looked like his lights weren't working, or something equally innocuous.

"But he's not even three!" he exclaims.

I shrug. "They're suspending preschoolers and kindergarten-ers all over the city these days, for 'bad behavior.' Guess what their race and gender are, mostly?"

Ballah sits down, puts his head in his hands. "During the war, things were hard, but we always knew that it would end, and then we would be able to do what we were supposed to be doing, in school, in our jobs, in our communities," he says. He is refer-ring to the twelve-year Liberian Civil War, in which more than 250,000 people were killed. "But here, I am starting to see that it is even worse than that. Because it is psychological. I see the boys in the park, the young boys, smoking and playing basketball when they should be in school. I couldn't understand why when I first arrived. Now, I am starting to see. It is because they have been told in school, in their community, on the street, that they are nothing, and so they have started to believe it. Once that happens, it is over. You can't be a man, a husband, a father. You can't do anything, once you start to believe that."

I nod, slowly. Then I walk up to him and put my hand on his shoulder. "We can't protect him from everything, but as his parents, we can still protect him," I say. "The good thing is that he's so young and cute now, and will be for a few years more. He won't grow into his full, Black male body for a little while yet. So we will still have a buffer zone until people will see him as a possible Black Male Thug first, Boisey second."

I turn around and look at my son, playing zombies with his friends outside. His laugh is infectious, and he just might be the most curious, good-natured person I have ever met. It is almost impossible to imagine someone being scared of him. But I know that day will come, and when it does, I want him to be safe.

———

But if there is a Fear of *the* Black Mother, there is also the equally punishing Fear of *a* Black Mother. This is the sometimes concrete, more often nebulous fear that those around you project, because they unconsciously believe you are unfit to mother your own child *simply because you are a Black woman*. It is the teacher who wonders how your child could not be potty-trained yet, the play group which is "just not a good fit" with the other middle-class white moms and their children, the story on the front page of the paper of the young Black mother who left her children alone in the park while she went to work at a fast-food restaurant and therefore had her parental rights terminated. It is the side eye you get from the shop clerk on the day you, like so many other mothers, have run out of energy due to exhaustion and raise your voice at your child after he will not let go of a toy you already told him he cannot have. The Fear of a Black Mother, not unlike the Fear of a Black Planet, has you " . . . *wonderin' why / People livin' in fear / Of my shade / (Or my hi top fade) / I'm not the one that's runnin' / But they got me on the run / Treat me like I have a gun,"* as Public Enemy so powerfully puts it. It is the already known, fully accepted truth that you are contaminated, damaged motherly goods, and that every mistake you will ever make while parenting (and like everyone, you will make many) was pre-ordained in the universal color and gender caste you grew into as a young woman: the Black Female Form. In the public view, your audacity to assume this body and dare imply that you are fully capable of caring for another small body, when by virtue of your own body it is clear that you cannot even take responsibility for your own, is tantamount to heresy.

With each loving, careful move you make through public space with your child, you are upsetting the natural racial and gender order of the universe and, therefore, blowing up people's minds right and left. With each impatient, angry move you make through public space with your child, you are reinforcing the natural racial and gender order of the universe, increasing people's fear of you and their desire to "intervene" on behalf of your child, who would, after all, be better off being parented by a "real" (read: white) mother.

No one wants to admit this, of course, but people *love* their fear. They love to see the world reflected back to them as they know it to be, and they love to know that there is something and someone else out there who is exactly the opposite of them: bad when they are good, mean when they are nice, irresponsible when they are selfless. If they didn't have this, then what would they have, exactly?

Mothering under these conditions is mothering under constant surveillance. It is accepting the fact that at all times you are either proving them wrong or proving them right. At no time are you simply building an ant farm with your child, or helping him learn to hold his breath under water. I don't fear that my child, or anyone else for that matter, will one day see me as *a bad mother;*

I fear that I will gradually and insidiously allow these uncompli-cated views of me as a human being to rob me of these moments with my son. That I will be so busy bracing for the next "hit" of bias or racism, trying to keep us safe and intact as a family, that I will not be able to be truly present with the very best, most in-nocent, most magical thing in my life: my son. Although the Fear of a Black Mother may never disappear from our culture, I need to find a way to resist it while not letting it over-determine how I engage with my child. Some days, I find that nothing is harder.

I am pregnant again, due in a month. It is a girl again, and I am terrified that she, like her sister before her, will not make it into this world alive. For any Black child to choose to come here, to this world, in these conditions, is extraordinary to me anyway. I think that is why my first daughter decided against it in the end. Perhaps she knew what dangers awaited her arrival. Perhaps she worried that my own Black female body could not save hers. In the end, I will never know, of course, and I am grateful to my son for giving me this chance to be his mother, to guide him along what I often fear is an increasingly dangerous path.

Because the truth is Black life—here, in this country, and here in Minnesota—is as contingent as it's ever been. No Black mother who looks away from this reality is doing her child a favor. But it is also a deeply intimate journey, a pact between mother and child that binds things that maybe should not be bound, like love and fear and acceptance and anxiety, and that transcends any facts that the outside world may claim to know. There is an inside to this experience of Black mothering, a sacred wholeness that is undeniable when I am within it. It is only the Black mother and her children who can embody it. Society at large, and whiteness especially, cannot conceive of it, much less know it. In the end, that is what saves us.

DISPARATE IMPACTS

Moving to Minnesota to Live Just Enough for the City

Taiyon J. Coleman

Although her first dream was to be a backup dancer for former hip-hop artist Heavy D, Taiyon J. Coleman is a writer, educator, and consultant, and her writing has appeared in numerous journals and anthologies. Currently completing her first novel, *Chicago @ 15,* she lives in Minneapolis with her family.

In 1998, I was accepted with full financial funding into two prestigious graduate creative writing programs: one at a university in the Deep South, and the other at a university in the North. I already knew that the artist Prince (my music boyfriend) lived in Minneapolis, Minnesota, so I decided to visit the city of Tuscaloosa, Alabama, in order to make my choice. What little I knew of the southern United States came from the *Eyes on the Prize*[1] documentaries and the Hollywood movie *Mississippi Burning.*[2]

---

[1] Like any good Catholic Black schoolgirl raised in the United States during the seventies and eighties with middle-class values without middle-class money, what I learned about drugs, sex, alcohol, and racism was through *ABC Afterschool Specials* and dramatic documentaries about slavery and racism of the southern United States. See *Eyes on the Prize: America's Civil Rights Years 1954–1965,* directed by Henry Hampton (Blackside, 1987).

[2] I saw this movie with my first boyfriend, my first love, who was also a Black nerd: chemistry major. At the time, we were both poor and first-generation college students raised on the South Side of Chicago. We're still poor. After watching this movie, we made a serious pact that we would never live below the Mason-Dixon Line. Eventually, I discovered that he cheated on me, we broke up, and when my mother died almost ten years later, he sent me a condolence card postmarked from Orlando, Florida. Traitor! *Mississippi Burning,* directed by Alan Parker (Orion Pictures, 1988).

As a native of Chicago, Illinois, I had lived almost the first two decades of my life on the city's South Side, always geographically above the Mason-Dixon Line.[3] Somewhere near the Ides of March, I set off on my tourist-and-idealist drive to southern Alabama. I blasted Chicago House music on the speakers of my red Hertz rental, and I drove alone from Sparta, Illinois, through the Mississippi River Valley heading south, with the explicit and repeated directions from my maternal grandparents to make sure that the car's gas tank was completely full and my bladder completely empty before I arrived at the Popeye Bridge.[4]

The Popeye Bridge crosses over the Mississippi River from the bluffs of Chester, Illinois, into the southwest part of the state of Missouri.[5] My maternal grandparents, who were born, raised, and came of age in southern Illinois[6] during the Great Depression, were not much afraid of escaped inmates from the Menard Correctional Center (formerly known as the Southern Illinois Penitentiary), which is located in Chester and home to notorious, diabolical, and insane criminals such as the American serial killer John Wayne Gacy. An entertainer by trade, Gacy "became known as the 'Killer Clown' because he lured his young unsuspecting victims into his home before killing them," and he buried the bodies within the concrete, walls, and crawl spaces of his home.[7] My grandparents were more afraid of the historical, ongoing, and de facto legacy of Jim Crow physical violence. They extracted yet

---

[3] John Mackenzie, "A Brief History of the Mason-Dixon Line," University of Delaware, 2005, accessed July 16, 2015, www.udel.edu/johnmack/mason_dixon/.

[4] So named to honor the creator of the cartoon character Popeye the Sailor Man, E. C. Segar, who was born in Chester, Illinois.

[5] The Show-Me State.

[6] The Land of Lincoln.

[7] The American serial killer and sexual predator was suspected of killing up to twenty-nine men and boys and burying the remains of the bodies within his Chicago-area suburban home. His neighbors complained of a distinct "smell" coming from his property, which led to his arrest. Gacy was executed by lethal injection in 1994. See Aamer Madhani, "Indiana Killings a Reminder of John Wayne Gacy," USA Today, October 21, 2014.

another promise from me not to stop my car for gas or a bag of spicy pig skins,[8] or to take a bathroom break at all in that part of Missouri until I (directly inside my car) passed the state line into Arkansas,[9] all before dark, and I set off.

From the time I crossed the Popeye Bridge into the state of Missouri, my grandparents had me all hyped up, looking for Ku Klux Klan members randomly popping out of the southern shadows at me, from the back seat of my rental car. I passed through the Missouri city of Cape Girardeau[10] and made my way to the state of Arkansas, where I stopped for gas and to use the bathroom. (I stopped compulsively glancing in my rearview mirror every twenty minutes once I left the state of Missouri.) From Arkansas, I drove through the state of Tennessee,[11] the state of Mississippi,[12] and finally into the state of Alabama.[13] I was a northern Yankee hot mess. A Black woman from the North in the Deep South for the first time, jacked up on cultural and historical knowledge from mass-produced liberal media primarily made of dominant and mainstream historical narratives and images of U.S. racism and waiting for something bad to happen.

As I drove along the outskirts of Birmingham, I knew the city was connected to important U.S. history such as the civil rights movement and the Birmingham bombings,[14] but ironically, I just

---

[8] Pig skins (fried pork rinds) taste better in the South.

[9] The Natural State.

[10] Birthplace to the Republican and conservative media icon Rush Limbaugh. I thought this fact might be useful in building tragic irony and satire in this essay. In the summer of 2000, when I traveled I-35 north in Iowa to teach speech communication at a local community college, I listened to Limbaugh on conservative talk radio, and I would laugh my ass off for the entire thirty-minute drive. There was no greater high! Man, I still remember that—that shit was really funny. I would hit the steering wheel of the car with my hand, never imagining that what Limbaugh was saying could ever really become mainstream. Guess who's laughing now?

[11] America at Its Best and/or Agriculture and Commerce.

[12] By Valor and Arms.

[13] We Dare Defend Our Rights.

[14] In 1963 a bombing at the Sixteenth Street Baptist Church killed four African American girls. See 4 Little Black Girls, directed by Spike Lee (HBO Documentaries, 1997).

imagined how from my car windows in the month of March, the city of Birmingham looked like any other American city from a red rental car speeding down and speeding south from the North on a federal highway. No one said, "Lookie here, girl," from the back seat of my rental car; no one tried to lynch me when I gassed up my car; no one tried to burn me on a cross when I used the toilet; and no one spit in my food and/or beverage (scene from *Roots*[15]) when I bought my meals from the fast-food drive-up windows (or at least I believe they didn't spit in my food; I guess I can't vouch for this one as pop/soda is carbonated and can easily conceal spit bubbles).

In less than twenty-four hours, I had made a solitary drive crossing five southern states in a red rental car from Hertz; the trip was really the plot for a bad but predictable misogynistic movie about a serial killer that preys upon single young females. Okay. I am not a White female, but close.

For the most part, by this time in my trip, I cued the House music to my internal soundtrack, and I thought to myself that attending school and living in southern Alabama for three years was actually possible. It was the turn of the century, wasn't it, and wasn't there a chance that I could be the Black Flannery O'Connor?[16] I was fifth-generation Roman Catholic on my mom's side,[17] and the Black stuff could be easily worked out. Just Details. Right? What was this *Eyes on the Prize* stuff about, anyway? If I extracted the occasional jolting southern accent[18] heard in passing through a rural gas station or from a fastidious and polite worker at a fast-food drive-through window, people and their

---

[15] *Roots*, directed by Marvin J. Chomsky, John Erman, David Greene, and Gilbert Moses (David L. Wolper Production, Warner Bros. Television, 1977).

[16] Flannery O'Connor (1925–64). White southern Catholic female fiction writer born in Savannah, Georgia. One of my favorite writers after Zora Neale Hurston, Toni Morrison, Alice Walker, and Nikky Finney.

[17] I now am a first-generation Recovering Catholic from over five generations (in America); I don't know what kind of Catholics my maternal line was before.

[18] It is important to note here that I am sure my city-slicker, fast-talking Chicago accent was equally as jolting to southern ears as well.

southern cities, through my eyes during my trip, seemed pretty much the same as cities and people in the urban North.[19] By the time I made it to the outskirts of the city of Tuscaloosa and to the university, I was convinced that my grandparents had totally hyped me up for no reason.

In southern Alabama, the flowers were in bloom, and the city was like a beautiful woman, my beautiful woman. After seeing her and smelling her for myself, how could any writer from the North, visiting the South for the first time, fail to make such a cheesy, sexist, and gender-constructing analogy for the beauty of the southern U.S. landscape in the spring? I was an urban northern city girl, and I saw colors and flowers that I didn't even know existed in nature. Some of the flowers were so huge to my urban concrete eyes that it was like they were from the movie *Food of the Gods*, without the gigantic killer rats.[20] I made my way to my motel, for which the university graciously paid. By the morning after my breakfast of bacon (real pig meat), biscuits, sausage (another type of real pig meat), eggs, syrup, and sweet iced tea (with no spit, guaranteed, I might add), I was sold on the southern life hook, line, and sinker![21]

Once on campus, I made my way to the department's graduate writing program, and I was greeted there by warm and sincere faculty members.[22] I thought they were all really nice and

---

[19] While a high school student, I worked at a McDonald's. My favorite job was working the drive-through window. The combination of customer service, speed, and accuracy was comforting. It was a world where everything worked right and made sense, especially if your cash register balanced at the end of the day. Please note that this was before automatic cash registers.

[20] Again, seventies and eighties television, while safe but not equitable, provided most of the cultural and folklore education for me and my sisters when we were not allowed to go outside. It was like a precursor to the "bigness" of the eighties. In *Food of the Gods*, the animals on a strange island grow to gigantic sizes; directed by Bert I. Gordon (American International Pictures, 1976).

[21] I am currently working on an essay titled, "Paula Deen, a Baked Potato, and Compassion."

[22] To my knowledge, there were no tenured Black instructors at that time in their graduate creative writing program.

thoughtful. There was one designated "Black Female Graduate Student" (BFGS) to "show me" around.[23] BFGS and I left the department to tour a little of the campus and to take a look around the city. I cued up my House music soundtrack on my internal twelve-inch vinyl record player, and the BFGS and I were on our way. In our enthusiasm, we were a little like Dorothy and Toto from *The Wiz*,[24] happily headed off to the Emerald City, once they had been assuredly pointed in the right direction.[25]

The first time the needle scratched clear across the twelve-inch vinyl was when I spotted the Confederate flag. Time stood still. I imagined that I must have passed countless Confederate flags on my drive from Illinois to Alabama, but for some reason, standing with the BFGS, this was the first time I had noticed it. I wondered if my perception of the South had changed because my physical position in the South was different—I was no longer a single solitary Black person.

When I stood with the BFGS during my visit to Tuscaloosa, she and I had formed a group. We had become more than one Black person within a physical space historically and contemporarily dominated by a structure of White male patriarchy, which depended on the historical invisibility, blindness, and silence of our Black and Brown bodies in order to continue to thrive and to survive. Like a flat balloon inflated by air, together the BFGS and I helped each other take shape and form. Our Black bodies became visible within a space where we seemed not to exist before. This

---

[23] Although this suggests the "show-me" state of Missouri, we were in Alabama.

[24] I need to stop here lest we become caught up in which one of us was the dog: me or the BFGS. It's *The Wiz* instead of *The Wizard of Oz*; it's in Harlem, not in Kansas, and I am in Alabama; Motown; Berry Gordy; Diana Ross; Diana means Goddess of the Hunt; somebody had an affair with somebody in power; this person did a gangster move, and then this person stole a movie part from a young blood (at the time); and, see . . . by that time, we lose focus. *The Wiz*, directed by Sidney Lumet (Universal Pictures and Motown Productions, 1978). *The Wizard of Oz*, directed by Victor Fleming and George Cukor (Warner Bros., 1939).

[25] This analogy might not work. Wasn't Glinda the Good Witch of the South, in the book? That's deep, y'all. See L. Frank Baum, *The Wonderful Wizard of Oz* (New York: Everyman's Library, 1992).

new visible space (our changed spaces) of multiplicity, visibility (being able to be seen), and our vision shifted our power as Black women and our power as Black people in that time and space. It triggered the ability for us to (seemingly) magically appear and to magically see, too, what we (I for the first time) hadn't consciously seen or recognized before: the big-ass Hollywood *Gone with the Wind* romantic movie version of Confederate flags all over the freaking city.[26]

My acknowledgment of seeing the Confederate flag in the physical presence of another Black body shifted our dimensional positions, our visibility, and ultimately it shifted my vision. I saw what I had not allowed myself to see before. What I once thought of as an attractive pretty lady, kind of like Glinda the Good Witch, was no longer a woman I wanted to be around, let alone love. The flags' visual presence worked to threaten us, to put us in our place lest we became too powerful, and all too clearly it conveyed the social, political, and racial ideology of the region, despite its luscious and decadent "womanly" spring welcome. I guess it was even worse since we (the BFGS and I) were supposedly educated (learn-ed) and free Negros: insert Frederick Douglass[27] here. I wondered if she, the BFGS, too, ever noticed the Confederate flags when she was just alone in Tuscaloosa by herself. Maybe BFGS had been desensitized, "caught up" in her ongoing solitary singleness. She was the only Black student in the program at the time. I looked at my new BFF, the BFGS.

"Are those Confederate flags everywhere?" I asked her.

"Yes," she said.

"Oohhh . . . kaayyy . . ." I said very slowly, and then I asked her

---

[26] *Gone with the Wind*, directed by George Cukor, Victor Fleming, and Sam Wood (Warner Bros., 1939).

[27] In Douglass's slave narrative, he notes that the first time he fully understood his oppression was when he learned to read, which further underscores why it was illegal to teach slaves to read and write. Slaves who have the capacity to fully see, comprehend, and communicate the structures of their own oppression were/are dangerous. See Frederick Douglass, *Narrative of the Life of Frederick Douglass* (New York: Dover Press, 1995).

what, judging by the look on her face, must have been the most stupid question on earth.

"Don't the Confederate flags bother you?" My eyes got really Diana Ross big, as I looked at the BFGS, searching for some sign of camaraderie.

"It's the South," said BFGS. The BFGS just shrugged her shoulders and seemed slightly annoyed with me. I guess I was ruining her Dirty South[28] soundtrack and the party by pointing this symbolic shit out to her.

I thought to myself that maybe I was overreacting; you know we Negroes from the North have been rumored to be historically problematic. So we walked to her car. BFGS preceded to show me, like a Black Vanna White, the sights of the campus and the surrounding neighborhoods of the university town where many students lived. The happy feelings from our first meeting in the morning had faded, as I now saw the Confederate flags everywhere. I couldn't stop and not see them if I wanted to. Confederate flags on cars, Confederate flags waving on tall poles in front of residential and public buildings, Confederate flags on T-shirts, Confederate flags on pens and pencils, Confederate flag diapers, Confederate flags on condoms, Confederate flag tampons and maxi-pads, Confederate flag bandanas, Confederate flag Band-Aids, Confederate flag earrings, Confederate flag wallets, Confederate flag underwear, and Confederate flags taped to car windows, bumpers, and license plates. I even found a brand of hot and spicy pig skins in a convenience store with Confederate flag packaging. My internal House music soundtrack wasn't coming back. I was tripping because no one was really freaking out about the Confederate flags, including the BFGS. I became jumpy, expecting a noose and a mob of folks covered in white sheets with guns to jump out at us at any moment. Clearly, I was the only one with the problem and most likely the one to be killed if we were jumped by a deadly race mob, or at least I would be the first one killed and killed slowly at that.

---

[28] No disrespect intended.

"Some folks I hang out with from the university are having a get-together this evening. Do you wanna go?" the BFGS asked and simultaneously changed the subject. She, too, could sense that the energy had shifted between us.

"At night?" I asked her. I don't know who has eyes bigger than Diana Ross, but this time, my eyes were bigger than Diana Ross's.

BFGS just looked at me and flared her nostrils. I almost thought I could hear her saying something about Black Yankees. She was so done with me.

I pumped myself up with an internal pep talk, as the twelve-inch vinyl to my theme song was completely scratched by now, and I just kept chanting to myself over and over again that it's just a flag. It's just a flag. It's just a flag. It's just a flag. It's just a flag. There's no place like home. There's no place like home. There's no place like home.

Once we looked at BFGS's apartment as our final stop on the city tour, we made our way to eat lunch, which was at a popular seafood restaurant chain, and my soundtrack was back in full force, as nothing takes my mind away from pain and trauma like food.

After lunch, the BFGS drove me back to campus. She was nice, but clearly our time was over. Looking back on it, I realize that in my explicit acknowledgment of the Confederate flag, I had revealed myself as a "certain type" of Black person, and my presence in the BFGS's sphere of identity production and existence in southern Alabama was not welcomed. I was a bad (not in a good assimilated way) Negro! The Confederate flags and the actual historical and structural racism that they explicitly celebrated and represented were not the problem. No, *I* had become the one who made it hard for the BFGS to exist and hide inside the solitary crawl spaces of White structural supremacy in Alabama. I wanted to say to her, "Dude. You are the one who is actually trapped inside the wall and not me. I'm free."

But instead, I was the disruption that scratched BFGS's needle across her twelve-inch vinyl record. I guess that if I wasn't with BFGS, the Confederate flags in Alabama did not have to exist, and with a bad Black person like me there, she would be in danger of becoming a certain type of Black person to herself and in the eyes of others.[29] With me not there, BFGS could be anything but a BFGS who was a descendent of African slaves, living and learning in a university town wholly and presently constructed as a result of cumulative historical and institutional structures immersed in the celebration of White supremacy and its histrionic historical narratives and symbols inside and outside of the university. Inside and outside of her, it seemed to pin her down, and I wondered could she feel it breaking through her skin.

I, my red rental car, and my judgment all made our way back to the motel for the night. The next morning, I left the university and its town for my northern drive back to Illinois. As I left, I knew that I would not attend the university. In my naiveté, I had thought before my visit that I could be comfortable with such explicit and conspicuous symbolic displays of White supremacy. As a result, I thought I had better options.

Shortly after I received my acceptance for a creative writing program for a university in the state of Minnesota,[30] a program instructor called me at home to personally persuade me to attend their program. Our discussion was warm, welcoming, and inviting, and ultimately I was flattered, honored, and excited about the wonderful possibilities of learning, creativity, and experience that I was going to learn, create, and have. After my spring break trip to Alabama, I thought that Minnesota was far enough north, and it was the home to my music man, Prince, so, of course, it definitely could not be as racist as Alabama. Right? I decided to attend the writing program in Minnesota.

Although my paternal granddaddy, Frank Coleman Senior, was born in Mississippi in the 1920s, it would be years before Grand-

---

[29] Not bad Negro or bad Black like *Spies of Mississippi* bad; those were some really badly constructed *bad* Negroes recently revealed from under the cover of darkness (pun intended). More like *Black Lives Matter* bad. It's the deconstructed Negroes who are the worst! See *Spies of Mississippi: The Campaign to Stop Freedom Summer's Civil Rights Movement of 1964*, directed by Dawn Porter (Trilogy Films, 2014).

[30] Land of Ten Thousand Lakes.

daddy would begin the ritualistic regurgitating of his young-man memories and retold stories of his forced leaving from the state, which bodily purged him at the age of fifteen under an immediate threat of a night lynching. In moving north from Mississippi, my granddaddy was following his mother and his younger brother, via the city of St. Louis, to the South Side of Chicago as part of his Great Migration.[31] Little did I know that when I decided to attend a university in Minnesota I would be continuing that Great Migration north and west. As Stevie Wonder put it, we were *living just enough for the city*.[32] Although I was nervous, I was extremely excited to finally be making my dreams as a writer come true in a place that I assumed was safe. By the time I had settled into Minnesota, I saw no conspicuous displays of Confederate flags.

All incoming students to the writing program were required, as a cohort, to take an introductory seminar taught by one of the established faculty members. As first-year students, we shared brief manuscripts in our genre with the seminar faculty and with our cohort classmates in a workshop over the duration of the semester. The seminar classroom was intimate and small, and all the students fit snugly around the table while the instructor sat at the head. One by one, the instructor discussed our various manuscripts in front of the entire class. As new students, we had this opportunity to introduce ourselves and our creative work to our program cohort, peers, and future career colleagues.

---

[31] See Isabel Wilkerson, *The Warmth of Other Suns: The Epic Story of America's Great Migration* (New York: Vintage Books, 2010).

[32] After raising five kids alone on the South Side of Chicago, my mother lost consciousness while talking on the yellow kitchen phone to her secret boyfriend in 1997. Eight months earlier, she watched me graduate from college, the first of her children and the first one in our family, on both sides, to do so. I walked across the stage in Ames, Iowa, and once I arrived on the other side, my momma greeted me and kissed me full on the lips like I was a little baby. By February, she was on life support. Stevie Wonder, my mother's music, got me through and helped me make sense of hard times, with both joy and pain, when she was no longer physically there to set me straight. Stevie Wonder, "Living for the City," *Innervisions* (Motown, Tamla Label, 1971).

"Tai, I read your manuscript, and there are numerous errors, and I think you need to take some grammar classes," the instructor said to me during class one afternoon, in front of all the students.

Some of my classmates snickered, and some of them just looked away, never making eye contact with me again for the entire semester, and some never made any eye contact with me for the remainder of the entire program.

"The characters in the poem are Black and urban, and they are using Black vernacular. They are from the inner city of Chicago. I am from the inner city of Chicago, and I write from some of my personal experiences and voices. This is one of the reasons I decided to attend a creative writing program, because I thought there was space to write like this creatively," I said back to the distinguished faculty, politely and proudly, without even thinking.

By the time I had started their graduate writing program, I had already completed a master's degree in English and had been teaching college-level composition for over two years in the United States and abroad. I wondered if the instructor had read my application, my application manuscript, and my student profile. I wondered if the instructor's statements were tied to the easiest point of reference for someone who showed up looking like me: Black, first-generation university student on both sides of my family, fat, urban, working class, and female. I guess I didn't look like the typical Minnesotan, nor did I look like the typical graduate student relative to the program's dominant student demographics. I definitely didn't look like the instructor, nor did I look like anyone in the seminar room.

"Well, you won't get published, then," the instructor said to me in a matter-of-fact tone that quickly quieted the room. The instructor's, the program's, and the institution's ethos in that moment depended on them being right and depended on my subsequent demise as a writer and as a Black woman writer. All my classmates, who had been out drinking with me the night before, quickly looked away, again.

There was no discussion of the content of my work: the themes, the characters, the style, and its legacy, position, and discourse within the canon of similar literary works and authors. In that moment, a constructed institutional stereotype had been tied around my Black neck like a loose rope with the threat of its threads tightening the more I resisted. If I stood my ground, the noose would only continue to constrict. If I gave in and assimilated, there might be hope for me, my work, and my neck. But then, in that moment with the criticism and stabbing words of that instructor, I was now just the racially constructed and undeserving Black Female Graduate Student (BFGS) granted admission to a competitive graduate program because of affirmative action policies. I wanted the carpeted floor to swallow me up, but I thought of my strong Black single mother instead.

I am the second oldest of five kids raised by a single mother. From the time I turned fifteen, I always had a job, in order to help my mother out. When I was in high school, I worked at a McDonald's in a western suburb near Chicago, which often required me to ride a bus one hour each way. At least once a week, I had to be a part of the closing team, and I would leave work at one in the morning on the bus. That one-hour bus ride became a cumulative two-hour trip home: a bus ride to the 95th and King Drive Station, a bus ride to 103rd Street, and a twenty- to thirty-minute walk home because the bus didn't run past my house at that time in the morning. Even with the illegal mace and stun gun that I always carried, it was a dangerous journey, but I had no choice if we wanted to eat, and if I wanted new clothes and underwear. During those times, my mother taught me to always look people directly in the eye whenever I was alone and walking in public, especially at night.

"If you think that they might try to steal from you or rape you, don't look away, Taiyon," she would say to me with a cigarette in one hand and a cup of coffee in the other.

"Let them know that if they come after you, that you gonna fight them hard, and they will decide that you are not worth the trouble and leave you alone." Sharply these words would leave her mouth, and then she would take a drag off her Winston cigarette and exhale smoke up in the air.

"Do you hear me talking to you, girl?" Momma would ask again, in response to my silence, to make sure that I heard her.

"Yes, Momma. I hear you," I would respectfully respond.

The memory leaves, and I am back in the intimate seminar room in the state of Minnesota with my esteemed instructor, but it feels like the corner of 103rd and Michigan Avenue on Chicago's South Side outside the liquor store and White Castle at two in the morning. I am walking fast and looking in all directions, one look after the other, to be prepared for an attack, but it is really the turn of the century, I am in Minneapolis, and the leaves outside the seminar graduate classroom are turning into fall. The instructor is looking at me and waiting for my response.

"Well, then . . . that's not a place where I want my writing to be published," I said, without even batting an eyelash while I dropped the microphone. A collective gasp could be heard throughout the room. My mother, who by this time had been dead for over a year, would have been proud.

It was only later, when I was taking the bus home from the university and walking from Nicollet Avenue to my apartment in South Minneapolis, that I felt the body pains that had grown into wounds from the instructor's well-intentioned words. It would be the first of many institutional scrimmages, microabrasions, and micro-aggressions that would plague my experiences as the only BFGS and writer within a predominantly White university writing program—a program that had generously funded my participation, a program that had attracted me and persuaded me to attend. But what I found and experienced instead within the university's walls was canonized book lists from majority core program courses taught by some instructors who failed to include any writers of color; being told by some faculty that any graduate student creative writing about race, ethnicity, and sexual orientation as subject and theme was "pat" and that race had already been done before, and it was exhausted, so please do write about new subjects and themes; some instructors advising me *that I* was racist if I wrote about race, and they sometimes forbade[33] the topic of race for seminar papers and presentations; being advised by some instructors not to expect favors, because clearly that is the only way I, as a BFGS, made my way through academia; never seeming to have the opportunity, as my White student program cohorts did, to develop sincere mentoring relationships with some instructors because they saw me and my work as something they could not or did not want to connect with and/or relate to; being advised by some instructors that it was inappropriate to talk about and to question the lack of equity in the program among instructors, curriculum, pedagogy, and students during program meetings where instructors had specifically asked for feedback from students regarding their experiences in the program; some instructors only discussing my writing in terms of sentence-level constructions and never in terms of its content and themes; and being told by some faculty that I should just focus on the mothering and raising of my recently born baby as opposed to advising me regarding next important professional options and steps upon the completion of a graduate degree in writing. However, the university willingly

---

[33] In a required graduate seminar, I proposed writing a paper arguing that the unnamed creature in Mary Shelley's *Frankenstein* was the literary construction of the nineteenth-century Enlightenment "nigger" in the text. The instructor denied my proposal, telling me that there had been a recent shooting and subsequent death of a White person that took place in a local neighborhood frequented by graduate students at the university. The suspected shooter was Black. The instructor told me that my paper topic and content would upset the White graduate student who had been affected by the shooting; thus, the instructor would not approve my paper topic and content. The instructor advised me that I was being racist and insensitive and asked me the question, with clear, physically shown frustration, "Why does it always have to be about race?" With compassion for any loss of life, I am still trying to figure out what the shooting incident had to do with me and my graduate work. The only thread that seemed to connect is that I was Black and the shooter was Black. The instructor, the graduate student, the murder victim, and Mary Shelley are/were White. Frankenstein's monster wasn't White. Mary Shelley, *Frankenstein* (New York: Vintage, 2009).

used my body's photographic images in its periodicals and publications and productions to demonstrate the welcoming environment and equity of its university and program.[34] Even the cheery photos, as sometimes I was placed with other Brown and Black marginalized bodies, didn't quite reveal how my body was painfully contorted to fit inside program spaces.

During my time attending the university, my Black body was meant to be embedded and hidden inside the walls, the crawl spaces, and the concrete of the university's institutional structures. My Black female body was not meant to be seen, to be acknowledged, to be heard, or to be discovered anywhere in my creative work nor within the program itself. Eventually, through my experiences, I discovered facts that I would only tragically realize later should have been of significance to my research selection process when choosing schools and places to live. In 2014, an online journal article ranked the state of Minnesota as the second worst state for Blacks to live, in the areas of home ownership, incarceration, education, and unemployment. Alabama did not even make it into the list's top ten.[35]

Unfortunately, these institutional experiences and impersonal policy and procedural points of institutional and structural inequity happen to all graduate students regardless of their identity positions and intersections within their respective institutions, but these daily micro-aggressions and microabrasions are disproportionally more damaging to marginalized bodies because of the legacy of our historical and institutional positions. Minnesota is now home to me and my family, and we have had

---

[34] Negro Teflon Deflector Shields (NTDS) up! My colleague and I, both Black women who teach at predominantly white institutions, joke that some educational institutions use strategically placed marketing images of their Black, Brown, and other marginalized-bodied members as deflectors, an obscuring agent, against any critiques (internal and community), discourse, and changes regarding equity.

[35] Thomas C. Frohlich, et al., "The Worst States for Black Americans," 24/7 Wall St., December 2, 2014, 247wallst.com/special-report/2014/12/09/the-worst-states-for -black-americans/.

great experiences here which we fully recognize, for which we are fully grateful, and which we fully value. There were supportive instructors, I have a great job (knock on wood), I exist and intersect within amazing diverse and dynamic communities, and I and my family experience our own intersections of privilege. But there has to be a place to voice the challenging experiences, too, in hopes of learning, creativity, and improving the experiences of others.

When I left my apartment that morning before the writing seminar, I was happy, the air was crisp, and the sun was bright in a blue sky free of clouds. From what I had assumed that day when I first woke up and looked out my apartment window, the weather would be warm. As a result, I wore a light jacket instead of something heavier. By the time I arrived at school, I was freezing my ass off, and I explained this to the department secretaries and janitors I had befriended, as they were much nicer and more welcoming than my classmates and some instructors. It seems that those of us who don't belong can easily recognize each other, and unlike the other BFGS, they didn't throw me under the bus. After my story of freezing cold in what was to be my first Minnesota winter, they all laughed at me and advised me that the coldest days in Minnesota are when the skies are the clearest pretty blue, amazingly sunny, and completely and beautifully free of clouds. They laughed at my ignorance in not preparing myself for the onslaught of the obvious cold weather. There was no bridge for me to cross, no state lines and/or multicolored flags to indicate that territories and ideologies had changed.

After enough microabrasions, I longed for the Confederate flags of the South, because at least the South had clear lines of demarcation and warning. In Minnesota, there were only smiling faces, open classroom doors, and a stinging persistent coldness that let me know that I was in a new, different place that wasn't really welcoming—and that this place was resistant to me calling it home. Later that evening, I crossed the Mississippi River on my way back to my apartment, and by the time I got to the building, I had to pee so badly that I had trouble unlocking the door. I made it just in time. As I sat on my toilet stool in absolute safety, I thought of the other BFGS—not the BFGS that I, too, had become—and I wondered, would she ever have attended a writing program in the North instead of attending a university in southern Alabama, if she had had the choice? Maybe she knew what I failed to realize during our short time together: there are Confederate flags everywhere, even in places where we can't see them.

A SURREALIST HISTORY OF ONE ASIAN AMERICAN IN MINNESOTA

David Mura

David Mura has written two memoirs: *Turning Japanese*, a Josephine Miles Book Award/Oakland PEN winner and a *New York Times* Notable Book, and *Where the Body Meets Memory*. His novel is *Famous Suicides of the Japanese Empire*. He's written four books of poetry, including *The Last Incantations*.

In 1974, I came to Minnesota for the PhD program in English at the University of Minnesota. There were very few Asian Americans here, and I was aware of that wherever I went, but in a rather unconscious way. I didn't think of myself as an Asian American or even as a Sansei, a third-generation Japanese American, much less as a person of color. I wanted to think of myself as an American, which was one embodiment of my desire to be considered white and, thus, in my thinking back then, normal, accepted.

I'd grown up in a white Jewish suburb of Chicago; I knew far more about the Holocaust and the concentration camps in Europe than I knew about the U.S. internment camps where my parents, as teenagers, were imprisoned during World War II. My parents never talked about the camps or said much about their parents (my grandfathers had returned to Japan after my grandmothers died and really weren't part of my childhood). As my mother later said, "We raised you to be an individual first, an American second. We really didn't think about the Japanese side of things."

To understand my mother's thinking on this, you have to realize that she and the other Japanese Americans were imprisoned in internment camps by the U.S. government simply because they were of Japanese ancestry, that is, because of their race and ethnicity. My mother was born in Seattle. She had never been to Japan, spoke no Japanese, and, at the age of twelve, was obviously not a security threat to the United States. No Japanese American was ever convicted of espionage against the United States. But though she was a natural-born citizen, she and other Japanese Americans weren't given the right to a trial—no writ of habeas corpus for them.

So what do you do if you are imprisoned for your race and ethnicity? The message is, *Those* are your crimes. And so my parents raised me with no knowledge of Japanese culture; they tried in various ways, consciously and unconsciously, to erase or play down their ethnicity. They couldn't hide their race, so they pretended it didn't exist. Somehow that seemed to work for them.

It didn't work for me. Despite my conscious denial of my ethnic and racial identity, I knew I was different; I sensed it. But the issues of race weren't there in the courses I was taking for my PhD; in my five years in the program, I read a handful of poems by Amiri Baraka and no other writers of color. And when my fellow PhD student, the African American poet Marilyn Nelson, handed me this anthology of Asian American writers, *Aiiiieeeee!*, I put it on my bookshelf and did not look at it for several years. For me, to read such an anthology meant I'd be somehow grouped with the writers within it, and I'd already learned implicitly and explicitly from my white professors and creative writing instructors that "minority literature" was called that for a reason: it was minor, secondary. To call myself a writer of color would be to relegate myself to a literary ghetto, to become part of an attempt to enter literature through a sort of back-door affirmative action program. It meant I couldn't cut it, couldn't make it the legitimate way, through the front door.

And oh, I so wanted to enter through that front door. I worshipped poets like Robert Lowell, John Berryman (who'd taught at the University of Minnesota and infamously jumped off the Washington Avenue Bridge), Randall Jarrell—all Ivy League–educated white male poets, wreathed in prestige and learning and tradition. They may have been tortured artists, but they were tortured in the ways white writers are tortured, by personal demons, by their families, by their sensitivity, by their fight against a barbarian mass culture. Race had virtually no place in their world, for to be white then, as it still is now for most white Minnesota writers, is to be without a race. This "race-less" status includes the privilege not to be seen as a "minority," as a sidelight, as secondary to the main thing.

But back then I hadn't read Fanon, I hadn't read Baldwin or bell hooks, I hadn't read Said or Aimé Césaire, I hadn't read Toni Morrison or Alice Walker—much less Maxine Hong Kingston or Frank Chin or the writers in the *Aiiieeeee!* anthology. I was so afraid of being tainted by the literary ghetto I knew they inhabited that I never went near such works. As a result, at least on a conscious day-to-day basis, I could avoid the questions of race that were already present in my all-white literary training and the all-white version of the Anglo-American canon I was being taught. When I went to my first big poetry reading in Minneapolis, at the Firehouse on the West Bank, I didn't think much about the fact that all the readers there—Robert Bly, Jim Moore, Patricia Hampl, Michael Dennis Browne, and Jill Breckenridge Haldeman—were white. I knew Bly from his first two books, from his magazine *The Sixties* (and then *The Seventies*), and I was aware of the quiet prairie surrealism that he and James Wright had helped make famous. Bly had been part of the antiwar movement; Moore had resisted the draft and went to prison for it. So politics was part of this literary scene. But ethnicity, race? These weren't part of the mix.

Where I couldn't avoid such issues, at least not to the extent I could in the literary world, was in the bars and nightclubs I went to—the Cabooze, and later clubs like Scottie's on Seventh, and Chi-Chi's out on 494 in Bloomington. For in clubs where people go in part to mingle with members of the opposite sex, the body—and thus, one's racial identity—is always present as an issue (whereas it can sometimes, though not always, be less prominent in situations like the classroom). I understood that there were black bars like the Tempo (now the Blue Nile Ethiopian Restaurant). But at the same time, I barely understood that there was something going on between the handful of black men who'd show up at the Cabooze and the white women there. I'd even overheard a white woman talking to her friend about the sexual prowess of black men, and I knew I was not a part of that, just as I was not white.[1] I had no knowledge of black life then, or black culture, and no black friends; to identify with the blacks in the club or to interact with them was not a possibility I entertained. I was too white-identified. So I didn't really think much about the black-white mix at the clubs I was going to.

On the other hand, there were no Asian or Asian American men in those clubs. If there was an occasional Asian American woman, usually a Filipina, she never paid any attention to me, never reacted to me as having any connection to her. If she was there, it was obvious she was there to look for white guys. The white guys knew this. They'd ask me if she was my sister, if I knew her, obviously hoping I might serve as some sort of sexual conduit.

Let me be clear. I did meet women in these bars, just as I met women in my classes or in interactions at the university, and all of these women were white. But clearly, in those places of sexual exchange, I was an anomaly. I didn't have a place. Oh, I could hide my face, my body, when I was studying Johnson's *Lives of the Poets* or writing a bad imitation of "Silence in the Snowy Fields"—but standing at the bar or asking a woman to dance as Lamont Cranston sang, "Don't roll your bloodshot eyes at me"? In the bars or clubs, I could never completely erase my awareness that I was not white.

---

[1] This is not to say, of course, that blacks back then had an easy time. In his memoir, *Incognegro*, my friend, the writer and scholar Frank Wilderson, describes how in the early 1970s the upscale Kenwood neighborhood in Minneapolis greeted his family, the first black family to move in: with a petition signed by five hundred people demanding that they be kept out. Frank's later attempt to date the white daughter of a former mayor was blocked by her family.

So I was caught then between two modes of processing my identity. In grad school, I could pretend I was raceless. But in the bars and clubs, I knew I was what I didn't want to be: a yellow man (here track Randy Newman crooning, "got to have a yellow woman when you're a yellow man"), a Jap, a Chink, someone associated with Mickey Rooney's yellow-face angry Japanese in *Breakfast at Tiffany's* or screaming soldiers being mowed down by John Wayne at Iwo Jima, or Hop Sing the cook in *Bonanza*, or the Chinese messenger who delivers the telegram to the gunslinger Paladin at the beginning of *Have Gun, Will Travel*. I was a weird anomaly, carrying the weight of stereotypes of which I'd been aware since childhood, constantly sensing that people didn't quite know what to make of me, knowing that people's reactions to me, especially those of women, were filtered through a lens I couldn't escape or quite deny. Since I was the only one, my presence wasn't seen as a threat, as an intrusion, in quite the same way that occurred when the immigrants from Southeast Asia arrived here.

Looking back now, I find my presence then could be viewed truly as an example of surrealism, what Bly later called "leaping poetry"—where an image from some distant or unassociated realm suddenly appears within the world of the familiar. But writing about that surrealism rather than Bly's "Silence in the Snowy Fields" or James Wright's poem about horses in a farm field outside of Rochester? My mind simply didn't go there. I had no context for the surrealism that was my actual life.

―――――

On innumerable occasions since that time, I've been in situations where I'm the only Asian or Asian American in the room. But certainly that's far less the case now in the Twin Cities at least, if not in the rest of Minnesota. When I think of myself as the only Asian American man at those bars and nightclubs, I'm struck by the sheer chutzpah I had then, the bravery, the audacity, and in some ways the blindness, that allowed me to stroll into those places and try to act as if I was no different than anyone else there, as if I were part of the norm and not an alien presence.

It's here that I come to a certain place of unknowing, a place that is, I think, an essential part of the Asian American experience. On the one hand, there are times when we as Asian Americans know clearly what non-Asian Americans, particularly white or black, think of us. Sometimes the thrust of antipathy and hate is quite palpable; at other times, we're aware that others think of us, "You don't belong here. You're a foreigner. An alien." (Such a sentiment can be expressed with a range of emotions, from hate to simply indifference or a lack of interest.) But while the stereotypes of African Americans are clearly present in the culture and are discussed constantly to contextualize news events involving blacks and race, the stereotypes of Asian Americans are not present or impressed in American culture and society in the same way. A lot of the time, other Americans don't think about us. We're invisible. We're not part of their consciousness, of the mainstream; we're not part of most discussions about race.

So what happens in the mind of a white or black person when they do encounter an Asian American? What stereotypes are brought up by our presence? What feelings or thoughts? What associations? American blacks have been dealing with whites and the issues of race for over four hundred years; they have a long history of interactions; they have developed a culture, a great culture, which incorporates and negotiates that history and brings it into the present and understands how the present comes out of that history and the role that race plays in both their history and their culture. But Asian Americans? Nothing in the culture of our ethnicity—whether it be Japanese or Vietnamese or Chinese or Filipino or Hmong—tells us anything about our situation in America, what it is like to live and interact with American society, nothing about how our bodies and faces affect the way people here view and deal with this or how such views and dealings affect the ways we look at ourselves.

I look back at that twenty-two-, twenty-three-year-old third-generation Japanese-American English PhD would-be poet grad student strolling through the Cabooze, some rhythm-and-blues band playing on the stage, and a crowd of mainly white young people and a handful of young black men, and I think of the night I saw Bonnie Raitt there, standing on some risers by the wall. And for a few moments, I thought of going up to talk to her and asking her to dance. In the end, I chickened out, probably in part because she was already (at least locally) famous.

In the annals of the Cabooze, still a local institution, who but me would even imagine such an encounter? It's unthinkable. It couldn't be part of Minnesota history.

And so it wasn't, though if I'd a little more guts, and I had talked to her, I have no idea what she would have made of it, what she would have made of me. My guess is that she would have politely turned me down, but what she would have been thinking about me specifically—as opposed to what she might have thought about any random white guy who would have approached her that night, which would have been something like, "I'm just here to listen to the music, pal. Why don't you leave me alone"—I don't know. My guess is she wouldn't have known either.

An Asian man walks up to Bonnie Raitt in a bar—that's the surrealistic image I should have been writing about, back then.

———

In the grand scale of things, my musings here aren't that important. My position, who I am, is still secondary, minor, a sidelight. I've lived in Minnesota for forty years. I've published four books of poetry, a couple of which have won national prizes. My memoir, *Turning Japanese*, won the Josephine Miles Book Award from the Oakland PEN and was a *New York Times* Notable Book. I've written another memoir and a novel and a book of literary criticism. But my books are never in the local authors section. Though I've won national awards for my books, I've never won a Minnesota Book Award.

Yes, I am known in certain circles. I am also infamous in others. Twenty years ago, the first time the Ordway Center for Performing Arts brought the ridiculous and racist *Miss Saigon* to St. Paul, I, and other local Asian Americans, protested the musical as well as the Broadway casting of a white actor in yellow face. I argued with white writer friends here about this yellow-face casting and the Orientalist stereotypes in the musical, and I then wrote an article about these arguments and my experience raising a *hapa* daughter here for the national magazine *Mother Jones*.

After that article was published, the community of white writers here reacted as if the Yellow Peril had risen up again. I got notes and letters saying things like, "Have you become a racial separatist?" and "Wendell Berry said the reward for destroying community is power" (to which I replied, "I think Wendell Berry was writing about huge agricultural corporations buying up family farms, and not one lone Japanese American writer arguing with a bunch of white writers about racial stereotypes"), and "Are you going to divorce Susie?" (my wife, who is white). Later, when someone brought up my name at a local university, my having written this article was cited as a reason for not hiring me. In the same conversation, one of my former professors said, "He dresses too well to be a minority." A local white novelist and essayist ran into my friend, the Japanese American poet Garrett Hongo, and told him what a horrible person I was for writing such an article. Garrett called me and told me I should be aware I was being attacked, not just locally but also at national writer gatherings.

To my white friends, I appeared to be a lone crazy angry Asian guy. But in 2013, the Ordway, deaf to the Asian American community for twenty years, brought back *Miss Saigon* for a third run. This time, the number of younger Asian American artists and activists who rose up against this piece of crap was larger, and far more organized, than twenty years earlier. When we held our protest in Rice Park in downtown St. Paul—as we had twenty years earlier—it was readily apparent that I wasn't necessarily the angriest Asian American in the state of Minnesota. Certainly, I was not alone.

And yet, the Ordway did not apologize to the Asian American community, nor did it promise not to bring *Miss Saigon* back.[2] Instead, it pointed to those portions of their audience—the white portion—that still see in *Miss Saigon* some romantic tragic tale.

So the 2013 protest in Rice Park of *Miss Saigon* and the Ordway is part of my history and also my family history. When my daughter was a small girl, around six or seven, I brought her, our oldest child, to one of the protests when *Miss Saigon* first came to town in the early 1990s. I wrote a poem about that experience; here is the opening of that poem:

Suite for Miss Saigon *(for my daughter)*

1. Prologue: Taking Samantha to the Protest
We're weaving through hard traffic this evening,
late for the plush new Ordway Theater,
the sky behind us sheets of palomino.

This is your second *Saigon* protest.
(Like Dracula, it keeps coming back.)
Why play this game again? a part of me asks.

This morning you read an essay I've written.
You ask why, as a boy worshipping Paladin
striding the hotel stairs, hipped with six-guns,

I never recalled the messenger hollering,
paper in fist, pig-tail flapping from out
his black beanie, "Teragram for Mr. Paradin!"

---

[2] Only more than a year and a half later, in the spring of 2015, did Ordway president Patricia Mitchell write a letter of apology to the Don't Buy Miss Saigon Coalition and the Asian American community. That letter came as a result of our demonstration, many meetings, pressure by the coalition and other Asian American organizations, contacts with local funders, and individual talks with Mitchell (in which I was a participant).

I try to explain. You nod, then say,
"I think that whites don't like to talk about race."
I look to your eyes, your sun darkened face:

Like Yeats' dancer, a blossoming bole
quickly unfolding, how soon your selves vanish.
Where is that girl in the pink pinafore,

replaced by one who sliced her Barbies in parts,
to be glued and stacked in installation art
protesting such simpering plastic ways?

Replaced by this tween in lime green, perusing
teen magazines, posting her wall with ads
for Skechers, *Felicity*, stars from WB.

Years ago, you asked why certain friends vanished,
those you recall, if at all, as strangers in photos,
vague figures in our kitchen or yard, laughing

as you waddled by or played your games.
Dear, here's how it happened. *Why* is more difficult
to say.

My daughter is now twenty-five. She's a principal of after-school programs and summer programs at a junior high in Oakland, California. She majored in college in critical studies in social justice. She's smart and capable, and she works hard at improving her school and the lives of her students. She knows how ridiculous *Miss Saigon* is, how it perpetuates the stereotypes of Asian women as sexual objects, exotic, constantly available. Another generation has passed, and still *Miss Saigon* plays at the Ordway.

This tells me how little has changed here in Minnesota in so many ways regarding how Asian Americans are perceived. We're still not part of the culture here; we're still aliens, foreigners. The attitude is part, "What are you doing here?" and part Orientalist fantasy, which it seems that so many white Minnesotans would rather encounter than real actual Asian Americans.

———

In the spring of 2015 I participated in a forum conducted by the Wilder Foundation about the issues of race and particularly the racial disparities that exist in Minnesota in education, health, income, employment, and more. The income disparity between blacks and whites here is actually greater than it is in Mississippi. And yet, we continue here to go around as if Garrison Keillor's Lake Wobegon conveys an adequate picture of who we are.

As people at the forum discussed why the racial disparities here are so great, given that this is supposedly a liberal state lacking the rampant and open racism of the South, here are some of the points people made:

1. The white people here are very white. To be white in Minnesota is different from being white in the South. A Southerner, whether a racist or not, knows that black people have lived in the South as long as white people; their history is intertwined. Whatever faults William Faulkner had in dealing with race, he recognized race not only as a central issue but as perhaps *the* central issue of his region—and indeed, our nation. There's not a white Minnesota author who even gets close to such a view. The issues of race don't exist in Lake Wobegon, and that's the way white Minnesotans want to think of their state.

2. The white people here don't like controversy or conflict. They like insisting that things are just fine. But in 2016 America, no one can discuss race without controversy or conflicts coming up, with tensions arising. So many white people here subscribe to the following tautological wheel: *The only time we encounter racial tensions is when the subject of race comes up. So the way to keep away tensions is to not talk about race. If no one*

*is talking about race, then that must mean racism no
longer exists.*

3. The white people here like to think of themselves as
   nice people. The idea that they actually might not be
   such nice people is so antithetical to their self-image,
   one feels their brains might actually explode if they
   even began to contemplate such a negative notion,
   such a critique of their own self-image. Again, that's
   not the view one gets from, say, Faulkner or Flannery
   O'Connor. The southern white author understands
   that evil exists and evil has existed in their world.
   They understand not only that the white Southerners
   are capable of being not nice but that they have been
   capable of great cruelties. But the Duluth lynching?
   That's an anomaly here. It's not really reflective of who
   Minnesota *was*, much less does it have any connection to what Minnesota *is*. Forget about Fong Lee, an
   unarmed Hmong man shot by police in Minneapolis
   in 2006. Or Chris Lollie, the black man tasered in the
   St. Paul skyway in 2014. Or the racial segregation that
   is still a substantial factor in Minnesota life (try to
   find a truly integrated house of worship in Minnesota;
   you won't run out of fingers counting).

I do understand that there is another side to white Minnesota. I do know that one reason why we've had such an influx of
immigrants in recent years is because, in many ways, these immigrants have found opportunities and support and a lack of overt
hostility that make Minnesota unlike other areas of the country.
But the racial disparities here still exist. And the Ordway brought
back *Miss Saigon* again. And I know I will never really ever be considered a true Minnesotan, despite my forty years here, despite
the three children I've raised here, despite all the art I've created
and participated in here. My relationship with the white writing
community here is still tangential, if not still antagonistic. My
son, who is of mixed race, still gets treated differently by the po-

lice, depending on whether he is perceived as a white kid or as a kid of color. For instance, when a group of my son's friends were in the park and a couple of them were drinking, the police came up to this group of eight whites and one other kid of color and my son. After the police frisked them, one police pointed to my son and the other kid of color and said to the white kids, "Why are you hanging out with those guys?" At a mainly all-black party my son was at, the police came, started frisking the black kids, and let the few white kids and my son go; one police said to them, pointing to the black kids, "Why are you hanging out with them?"

So why do I stay here? I stay because I love the people of color here, I love the artists of color here. In 1992, I worked with a number of local Asian Americans to start the Asian American Renaissance, an Asian American community arts organization. During the inaugural conference of the AAR, at a party at my house, theater artists Rick Shiomi and Dong-il Lee started a conversation about creating an Asian American theater company here, and the two became the co-founders of what is now called Mu Performing Arts. In the years since, the Twin Cities have become a center for Asian American art and artists (Mu is the second-largest Asian American theater company in the country).

In part because so many of us artists of color here still feel shut out from the mainstream, so many of us feel unrecognized or under recognized, we don't see art as a refuge from or as separate from political and racial concerns. And especially among the Asian American artists here, we're more openly pissed with the status quo; we're more up front about our identity and issues as Asian Americans than places where there are more substantial numbers of Asian Americans, as in parts of California.

Beyond that, because of the smaller size of the communities of color here, there seem to be more reasons for and impetus toward coalitions, working together, seeing our common interests, understanding that if we fight together—rather than battle each other—we'll be stronger, more effective, more likely to be heard. When we held an open forum on *Miss Saigon* at Minnesota Public Radio, Sarah Bellamy, co-artistic director of the Penumbra

Theatre in St. Paul, spoke eloquently and passionately about how the issues brought up by *Miss Saigon* are the same issues that African American artists face—stereotypes, marginalization, cultural erasure, the inability of white Americans to listen to a story where a white American is not at the center, the lack of appreciation for the artistry and history of people of color. It didn't matter to Sarah that we were talking about *Miss Saigon* rather than, say, *The Scottsboro Boys* or *The Help*, or the lack of writers and directors of color at the plays the Guthrie puts on. She could see we were engaged in the same struggle.

—————

A few years ago, I was asked by the *Nation* to write about Minnesota for an anthology, *In These States*. When they invited me, I was a bit surprised that they didn't ask someone like Garrison Keillor or Patricia Hampl or Charles Baxter or Jim Moore or Louise Erdrich. But then I realized it wasn't someone from Minnesota who was doing the inviting; it was someone out of the state, and they knew me as a writer with a national reputation, and it was far more likely for someone outside this state to associate me with Minnesota than someone inside this state to see me as a representative Minnesota writer.

In the 1930s the *Nation* did a similar anthology. Langston Hughes wrote about Georgia; Sherwood Anderson about Ohio; Edmund Wilson about New Jersey. Sinclair Lewis, in his essay about Minnesota, talked about the strange new immigrants the Swedes. Most white Minnesotans have forgotten that they were strangers here once. Or that they are not native to this land.

One night at the Cabooze, back in the seventies, a Native American woman started talking to me, and she asked me to go with her to a Native bar on Franklin so she could show me her people. When I was younger and had long hair, there were times when Native Americans mistook me for Native, but this obviously wasn't the case, since she used the phrase "my people" and not "our people." Still, I sensed she wouldn't have asked someone white to do this. So we went to Mr. Arthur's on Franklin, and though at the time I was wont to make a pass at almost any female, I didn't with her. The reasons for that are complicated. Partly I was enamored then of white women, but it was more than that. I felt in her a yearning for me to really see her and the other Natives at Mr. Arthur's, a yearning that was larger and more profound than anything sexual between us. And perhaps some part of my stupid young drunken asshole brain knew that her bringing me to that bar was an honor, that I shouldn't desecrate that.

Years later, I would read Sherman Alexie's wonderful story "Class," where a middle-class Native Spokane lawyer, with a troubled marriage to a white woman, visits a Native bar in Seattle. He's never done this before, but the trouble in his marriage has awoken inside him a desire to connect with other Natives. So he goes to a bar much like Mr. Arthur's. There he gets in a fight with a Native man, Junior, who instantly sees the lawyer as a bleached-out yuppie, an intruder into the world of the bar, and when the lawyer wakes after the fight, he's being nursed by the Native woman bartender, Sissie, and the lawyer makes a drunken pass at her. Sissie is appalled and says something like, "You asshole, you think because I'm poor and ugly I'm just going to sleep with you." But I want to be with my people, says the lawyer. We aren't your people, says Sissie. You left our world a long time ago. You want to be in our world? Do you know how much me and Junior want to be in your world?

Back when I was twenty-two, I hadn't read Sherman Alexie or Leslie Marmon Silko or Louise Erdrich; I knew no Native Americans. I had no context or understanding then of the Native community here. In many ways, I still don't. In many ways, I am still the asshole yuppie lawyer I chose never to become, bemoaning my middle-class troubles. I am the tourist, invited in by a Native woman who knows deep in her heart I'll never see what she sees, that in that bar all I'll see is a bunch of Native people drinking. A stereotype. Which told me nothing. Which told me everything.

And yet I do see that Native woman in ways I didn't before. I know I'm an intruder here, an invader at worst, at best a guest.

As a guest, I have my own work to do about making this community of all of Minnesota more inclusive, more aware of its history, more aware of the history taking place right now in the present. I have to still acknowledge the yuppie asshole lawyer in me, the part of me that has always lived in the white world, in that comfort. That still wants that comfort. That still thinks I'm something, that white disease.

I have to keep working. That's all I can do.

WITH AN "E"

Venessa Fuentes

Venessa Fuentes is from the Twin Cities. She is also from its arts, queer, and POC communities. Her writing has been anthologized, read at poetry picnics, shared at the dinner table, and turned into public art. Along with her son and her wife, Venessa claims the south side of Minneapolis as Home.

Let's say you are a brown girl. One who is born in 1974 suburban Minneapolis. And, for various reasons having to do with your parents, let's say you are raised primarily by your abuela who speaks Spanish. Probably the first thing you will notice is how different you are in almost any setting. You are different in school because most of your classmates, as most residents of 1980s suburban Minneapolis, are White. You are different from your mother's family because you are the Black girl. You don't spend as much time with your father's family, but when you do you are different from them because you *aren't* the Black girl. These are absolute truths. Like gravity working on the body, like the unique signature of each snowflake that has ever fallen: you clearly will never be the White girl; are not entirely the Black girl; and are not 100 percent sudamericana.

So what, though? you might rightly think to yourself, as a brown girl in 1980s suburban Minneapolis. Aren't all of these girls different, depending on where they are, too? Aren't all girls *just* girls? Just, you know, *girls*. Girls who ride Big Wheels, who eat bologna sandwiches on white bread with mayo, who wear their hair in pigtails. Rule-following, daydreamy girls. Just like you, you might suppose, they walk to the Red Owl with their abuelas for the week's groceries. They search for the smoothest stones, count and name individual cherry blossoms up and down the perfumed length of Shingle Creek. Right? Sure, you will have an occasional moment of second-guessing all of this supposing. But that is when, refocused, you insist that *If these girls are anything like me, they like to go to 31 Flavors for chocolate peanut butter ice cream cones.* They surely watch Scooby-Doo after school and the Smurfs on Saturday mornings. They love to swim with their friends in the apartment complex's over-chlorinated pool while all the moms drink pitchers and pitchers of frozen strawberry daiquiris. Right. This, you claim, is the absolute truth of Girlhood. And, so far, it's good.

The next thing you will most likely notice, now that you know the baseline, the entry point of how different you are in almost any setting, is how you find yourself wondering about what's up with being different. About why it matters. *Is it just me,* you wonder to yourself, *or do there seem to be different kinds of being different?* Remember though, you are a girl and not a grownup at this point in the story. You don't get all deep about why being different matters; the big questions haven't started quite yet. They haven't elbowed or clawed their way into your air space. For today, you are early to the wondering game. You are just beginning to pick up on how there are different kinds of different.

How might you explain all of this to someone, then? Let's say an adult in your life, a teacher or a frozen-strawberry-daiquiri-drinking neighbor mom, asks you to draw the different kinds of being different. This will be easy-peasy since you love drawing, and so you get straight to work. You start by dividing the page in two. On one side of the page, you draw cotton ball clouds, deep green grass, and a candy-colored rainbow. Maybe there are a few pink and purple hearts floating around in the sky, near the lemon yellow sun, for added effect. On the other side of the page, you draw gray skies, patches of thorny grass, and broken hearts. Some of the heart pieces float around in the sky, some have fallen into the dirt, and others are tangled up in the thorny grass. Finished, you explain to the adult, bright faced and matter-of-factly:

See? One kind of different is nicer and one kind of different has sharp edges. Absolute truths. No big questions yet.

Later that night you have brushed your teeth and are all tucked in. As much as you love chocolate peanut butter ice cream and over-chlorinated swimming pools and walks to Shingle Creek with your abuela, this is your most magical time. The quiet routine of getting into bed brings you a lot of joy because this is when you get to release the day's collected daydreams. You let their company fill up and secure the room, line the cool bedsheets. Their constellations reveal stories that help you fall asleep. Sometimes you hum to yourself. Sometimes you can hear your abuela praying her nightly prayers in the next room. Sometimes if she is praying, you send out your own sincere thanks for this best, most joyful part of the day.

Tonight, though, the routine is different because you have officially noticed that there are different kinds of different. *And* you increasingly wonder about them, about why that should matter. The day's daydreams catch up to you in a way they haven't before, which is, unbeknownst to you, how the wondering game works. You wonder about that picture you drew earlier in the day. About where your place is in that picture. Then it happens: you wonder *Maybe I am surrounded by sharp edges.* It occurs to you that you have felt them when the girls at school—the same exact ones who want to play with you at recess and crown you as their bestest friend—sometimes call you silly names that call out your different skin color. Sharp edges have snuck up on you when cousins from both sides of your family—the same ones who eat birthday cake with you or bring you really cool presents at Christmastime—make tiny comments or toss little side eyes at you. Now that you are really wondering, you remember how sharp edges surprised you when your mother, who normally lets you swim all day long every summer, said *Stay out of the sun. I don't want you getting too dark* the week of your cousin's wedding.

You lie there, all tucked in, with a disrupted nighttime routine. A line of second-guess questions crowd out your constellation of

daydreams: *Am I making it up, or did my cousin really give me little side eyes? If my friend says she was just joking then why wasn't I
laughing? Is it just me or do my tios and tias like me less because I am
darker? How come the people that like me best let those sharp edges
into the room?* You have just crossed a threshold, stepped into new
air space. The big questions, at this point, have begun. As have
their unkind elbows and claws. You need a moment to adjust. You
don't realize when a bit of your bright face goes out.

Second-guess questions make you want to find answers. Like
when you work on math problems. You want a new set of absolute
truths. Maybe, then, you are surrounded by sharp edges because
you are an only child. Right? Or maybe it's because you are shy
and, instead of joining in during rowdy basement dance parties,
prefer to watch your mom, tios, tias, and cousins from the sofa's
anchor point. Or maybe you are surrounded by sharp edges because you are the only Vanessa in the world who spells her name
with an "e." Now that you have crossed a threshold, whatever the
answer, there is an entirely new kind of being different that has
disrupted you. They occupy you now, all the time, those edges.

Occupied, you start the next day thinking even more about
where your place is in that picture. That picture, of course, being
the world. The world, of course, being 1980s suburban Minneapolis. A mostly White world that includes occasional trips to the
Black and Bolivian spaces of your family. Each increasingly
troubled brain scan shows you that your world is a White space:
the TV shows you watch, the books you read, the Barbies you play
with. Your world is of and for the girls you are growing up with.
Just, you know, *girls*. Girls who totally like the same things you
do, who are your friends. But they are also consistently shining in
the brightest, prettiest spotlights. They fit everywhere they go—
as they eat bologna sandwiches and run to the grocery store—
because it is easy; they don't really have to think about it. And why
would they? It's just a sandwich, just a trip to the grocery store.

It is as if the world's enterprise is to cheerlead on certain kinds
of girls while giving you an intermittent wave—one you could
almost mistake for shooing a fly away or something like that. It

is as if the world is broadcasting secret signals that give certain kinds of girls full permission to be themselves while giving girls like you boundaries to watch for and checkpoints to observe. And, because this is the world's enterprise, it's normal for both kinds of girls. It's okay. You don't ever hear your friends say *I hate you because you're a brown girl, Venessa!* If anything, you get invited to their parties and sit together on the school bus because they really like you. Because you really like them. Because 1980s suburban Minneapolis is still full of chocolate peanut butter ice cream and over-chlorinated pools.

In response, you make impossible brown-girl wishes to fix the problem. The problem, of course, being you. *If only*, straight hair. *Please*, light skin. You pause briefly to remember your mother's warnings to stay out of the sun, and then get back to work. You wish for things that could make you more normal: brothers, sisters, a totally different name like Angela. Or something tomboy-ish, like Samantha-Sam-for-Short. Knowing that none of these wishes will come true, you concentrate on what you can fix. The Spanish-speaking part is the first to go. By age seven your mother tongue, the one that traveled to Minneapolis all the way from La Paz, Bolivia, in 1960, will only be spoken at your abuela's. By age ten you know how to read and respond to the bodies and rules—both spoken and silent—in a classroom, on the playground, at a birthday party. Luckily, by age fourteen you discover the gift of words, how they spin the warm company of your routine daydreaming into a valuable tether. You write poems and journal about how simultaneously frustrated and thankful you are for the internal skill set that tells you what parts of yourself you need to minimize or amplify depending on the setting. By the time you are a seventeen-year-old brown girl who is familiar with the "It's Really Nice to Meet You, Dear! I'm Not Racist, but Please Don't Date My Son, and Pass the Tacos I Just Made in Your Honor" look nervous mothers emit when their sons bring you home for the first time, this is all second nature. It's a normal and okay problem.

Long gone are the Days of Absolute Truths. Now you know

how much it costs you to be in your brown girl body. Just to have your place. You do not have full permissions, you can only day-dream about how certain kinds of girls must move through the world. Sometimes when you are feeling particularly observant, you suspect they pay a price, too. Which then makes you think that the world's enterprise must extend beyond just girls. You wonder about certain kinds of boys, what prices they pay in their bodies. About who ultimately is in charge of setting these curren-cies. About how that role was assigned. Or taken. Or inherited. It occurs to you that your mother, abuela, and everyone else before you—people who lived oceans and ages ago—certainly would have paid for the places in their bodies. And then it almost be-comes too much, the mental hum of you thinking about how the whole world is in on this.

After years of noticing, learning, and writing, you will natu-rally want to get away from most of suburban Minneapolis as soon as you graduate from high school. A confusing, privileged mixture of the sharp edges that surround your brown body actu-ally help get you into college. You are two kinds of Not White *and* a female, so lots of colleges want to add you to their lecture halls. Their scholarship forms, eager to know which box you fit into, ask *Choose One*, and you are deflated when you see that one of the first options is *Black, Non-Hispanic*. Your second nature, remem-ber, is to second-guess question yourself, which you do as you fill out these forms. You are certain that it's only the box you check and not your grade point average and exquisitely written essay that will be considered. Words like *diversity* and *multicultural* become a spotlight in your face, behind your back. And this spotlight is not at all like the bright, pretty kind of your young girlhood. Meanwhile, you are a first-generation student whose family wants progress, so they want you to go to college. And why shouldn't they? A super-nice liberal arts college in St. Paul is where, fortunately, you are accepted. This is Young Womanhood: You are supposed to graduate from high school. You are supposed to go to college and graduate in four years. You are supposed to get a job. Your best friends are supposed to be girls, you are supposed to date boys, and one boy is supposed to ask you to marry him. This is the world's enterprise.

Your college years turn out to be some of your best. Yes, you are surrounded by mostly White kids (nothing new) whose parents write huge tuition checks every semester (totally new). Yes, you struggle with which student organization to join: the one for Black folks or the one for Latinos? Yes, you go home every weekend instead of staying on campus because you are shy and, instead of joining in during rowdy basement dance parties, prefer the familiar tether of your suburban Minneapolis anchor point. But at a particular moment, let's say as a second-year student, you dig into college. You take Women, Race, and Class: An Introduction to Women's Studies. That leads to a Feminist Perspectives in Anthropology class. African American Women Writers. Women in Art. Exile in Women's Writing and Film. You join the Women's Collective student organization and, when you're not lost in stacks of books at the library, you write stacks of poems. You declare yourself a Women's and Gender Studies major. As your senior year begins you find a roommate, move off campus, and visit suburban Minneapolis less and less. It is 1996. You are generally less troubled in this new air space because you are more you. On graduation day, dream job lined up, you are just as aware of the sharp edges that surround you. But you ignore them, feel liberated, and see nothing but potential. This is the closest you have ever felt to fitting in, which is striking. It is striking because you have managed to find it only by going to a private undergraduate liberal arts college and immersing yourself in all of its privileges. It is as if you have had a temporary passport full of permissions.

Now. Imagine how struck you will be when your future self meets you for a cup of coffee and says, *Next year you will meet a man at a poetry reading. He will charm you with a bright force of kind words. You will immediately move in with him and burn through bottles of beer, glasses of wine, and notebooks of poems. It will be fun at first. Then you will ask him to move out when all of that drinking gets in the way of everyday living. He will move out, get sober, and ask you to take him back. And you will, repeatedly, for close to ten years. Each time will feel a little worse than the last. Your friends, your mother will applaud you when he moves out, only to slouch over when you take him back. I have come to prepare you, Venessa with an "e." You are gradually going to lose track of yourself. All those sharp edges you constantly feel surrounded by? They will fade into the background, pale in comparison to what this person is going to surround you with. Confusing cycles that start out* I need you and I promise I am a better person for you *and end* By the way you fat dummy, I still love you. It serves you right to suffer *will become normal. So normal, in fact, that you are going to marry this person and have a baby with him. I am here to tell you that your son will help you find your way out. But not without you leading the fight of your life, and not without significant damage to your well-being. It will take you years to see yourself, to be kind to yourself again. Get ready.*

But, of course, there is no meeting with your future self. Not even a predictive dream or a tarot reading. And even if there is, you are not going to have any of it because you are a Women's and Gender Studies scholar. A self-identifying Feminist Poet of Color who was raised by an abuela who left an abusive marriage in Bolivia. And everyone else before you, people who lived oceans and ages ago, fought to survive for their freedom and their place. They paid for you to be here today, just like you are paying for everyone else after you. You are not going to have any of it because nobody else pays your bills, manages your schedule, or tells you what to do. See? You are not in danger of losing yourself. Then, one day, you go to a poetry reading.

You end your confusing marriage nearly ten occupied years later. All you wanted was to fit into Young Womanhood and all its potential, but you reverted. It is at this moment, tetherless and disrupted, that you are ready to be more you again. Ready for real normal. As you turn the corner, your ten-, twenty-, thirty-year-old ghosts and their needs will follow you. Make it their business to disrupt, elbow, and claw. They will work against your every step. But, as you did before, let's say you ignore them, feel liberated, and see nothing but potential. You clear a new air space for yourself and your son. One that will not be ruled by a manipulated picture of love. Not for another abusive moment. Never again.

Let's fast forward a couple of years. Your son is three, you make a good life in present-day Minneapolis. You write poems again. About ghosts. About living brightly. There have been a few dates. None of them know your life's details; you don't tell them about your son. You promise yourself that he will remain off-limits to dates until the time is right. And after a few more dates that go nowhere, you are happy to take a break instead of falling into ghostly cycles. Which is exactly the moment when you meet her. You have just crossed a threshold. And everything is right, which is striking. There is a flood of everything right, of full permissions, with her. You are ready to see her and be seen by her. You want her to know your life's details, especially all about your son. With her, you want to do all those Young Womanhood things you were supposed to be doing all along.

For the first time, you are beyond the basic math of being more you. For the first time, you are the whole, Absolute Truth of You. It feels unmistakably better. It is as if you no longer have to wonder where your place is in that picture you drew back in the day. As if you know that being surrounded by the world's sharp edges will still cost you, that they will always want to occupy you with their elbows and claws. Only now, there is an entirely new kind of being different that has, for the first time, disrupted all of them. And that's probably the best kind of different you have noticed in a while.

TROUBLE IN MIND

To Be Black Is Blue in America

IBé

IBé is many things, and they all orbit around being father to his son and daughters. He lives in the Middle of the Atlantic, hoping his children make it to America (without leaving Africa behind). He writes poetry and passes it off as spoken word. Or maybe it is the other way around.

Sometimes I catch myself staring at my son, wondering what he is going to do when someone gives him a piece of paper with boxes on it and asks him to check the box saying who he is— if he is going to pause before marking "Black." As I do. Because lately, I have been thinking that although America tries to make it so, Black is not a race. They call it "race and ethnicity," but it cannot be ethnicity, either. I was raised in Sierra Leone, I know ethnicity. I grew up Maninka among Fulas, Kissis, some Temnes and Limbas. Each group spoke a different language, had varying customs, and was known to be predominantly one religion or the other. The last I checked, both Black and White Americans speak the same language. English. This is not my language. They are mostly Christians and celebrate Thanksgiving the day before Black Friday. If a color was associated with a day, before November 1991, my Fridays were symbolized by the white garments most of us wore to mosques on these days.

If Black, like White, is not a race, then it must be a classification. And as with all classifications, there must be a shared characteristic among all members of this group. Certainly this shared characteristic cannot be skin color. There is a wide range of skin color in what America considers Black. In fact, when it comes to the box, some with black skin are not allowed to check the "Black" box. Instead they are told to check the "Hispanic" box. North Africans should mark "White," and children of Black and White parents—with white skin, sometimes blond hair and matching freckles—mark "Black." It cannot be geography either. Otherwise, American citizens of Haitian origin cannot be expected to mark "Black" while those of Dominican origin are asked to mark "Hispanic."

So what is it? What makes one man "Black" and the other not? I thought this characteristic, this qualifier, had everything to do with slavery. American slavery. So where does that leave me—a son of Africa whose family history has never been bound in chains, whose route to America was thirty thousand feet *above* the Atlantic Ocean, with a name passed down from many generations before? In 2011, I went to our hometown in Kankan, Guinea, where my father's house is still standing, down the road from where his father's house stood, a few miles from where my great-grandfathers lived, all the way to Kabalaba, the very ground where my great-great . . . grandmother gathered her sons after a long journey from the heart of the Mali Empire and set down the guiding principles of this new land they were to call home. As happened with other so-called discoverers, when we got there, there were already people living on the land, but we took it from a wilderness and made it into the city it is today. (This may be very conquistador of me, but Maninkamoris do not negotiate their claim to Kankan. Blame it on my heritage.)

But I was wrong. Though Black is American made, slavery has very little, if anything, to do with it.

Before America, I was not Black. I was not adrift in a sea of White that I constantly had to come to terms with, against which my very humanity is measured—by Whites, Blacks, the world, and even myself. You see, Black exists only because America is White. There is no denying this. Just as there is no denying the fact that America is Christian. Your political leaning might encourage you to wish it away; those in power may even try to legislate it out. But the truth remains: America needed civil rights laws because she is White and Protestant.

Before moving to America, I did not see the world through a "Black" lens. Koindu, that small town in eastern Sierra Leone, was all black. In other words, was not Black. (Just like Kankan and many parts of Africa.) We had doctors, teachers, wealthy men. Indeed, we had successful men of all stripes. We did not have Black doctors, Black businessmen, or any so-called role models. We had people doing things we children knew we could just as easily do when we grew up. The town had a few drunkards. We laughed, teased, and threw stones at them as they stumbled through the neighborhood. Some of our fathers could not feed their families. We did not aspire to be like them. Though many of our parents studied the Qur'an (at home or under the tutelage of a neighbor or a makeshift madrassa), most of them never set foot in a European-style school. But they insisted that we did. The police chief and all his deputies were corrupt and sometimes cruel to our mothers at the marketplace. Those with power are prone to abuse it. This may just be human nature.

The two churches with lavish compounds had two white men for priests. We hardly saw them outside of those compounds. A white person or two would appear on a Market Day. We thought they were peculiar. Especially when they put peanut butter in their baguette and ate it.

Sight is about contrast. You cannot see an object if there is nothing to contrast it against. Reality works in the same way.

When I first got to America, I did not see me any differently. I saw many new things, including more white people than I knew existed. But that was just an observation, like seeing a penguin for the first time. What I needed—what would come later—was a sort of out-of-body experience. To not only see my surroundings, but to see me in them.

I could not see how I looked next to Whites, indeed among Whites. More importantly, I could not imagine how these people may be seeing me. Needless to say, when racism snarled its teeth, I smiled back. When I veered from my almost-Evanston Skokie neighborhood into Skokie proper, where a "neighbor" thought I stole the bicycle I was riding and followed me all the way home so I could prove to him otherwise, my uncle thanked him. (Although he had been in America nearly twenty years at the time, my uncle, too, was raised outside of the American experience.) When a teacher handed me one of my first tests with a smile and words I remember as congratulatory, I was shocked to later learn what "D" represented. You may think that is not a big deal, that a teacher is supposed to make the student feel good no matter their test score. I would tell you it is about expectations—if little is expected from someone, everything is a win and a cause for celebration. We are wired this way, as human beings; when the goal is low, most of us fall to it rather than set our aim beyond. This may just be one of the situations plaguing Black students' achievement. A "B"-average Black student is toasted as one other students should admire and look up to. So a "D" Black student looks at this and forgets that "A" is the goal; therefore, when he gets a "C," he thinks that's not too bad, because it is just a step below a "B."

But just give it some time. If your skin is dark, sooner, not later, you will be "Black in America." It was in St. Cloud, Minnesota, where I slowly went from black to "Black in America," where I first started sensing something was afoot, that my color was starting to shape my experience. I cannot pinpoint the exact moment. Maybe it was that time, two weeks after I moved there, when a car slowed down next to me as I walked from downtown back to school, perhaps so the driver and passengers could take a closer look at me, to see if I was real and not an apparition from their teevee. Or the following summer, when the police stopped me on my way home from my cousin's, three blocks away, because I had some CDs in my hand and they had "received a call about someone breaking into an apartment." Of course they wanted to know where I was coming from, where I was going, who gave me those CDs, do I go to school, could I take them back to my cousin's. . . . Or maybe it was a year later, when in a stupid altercation outside a bar, a drunk White boy called me a "Nigger" and I hesitated for a moment, because really, to the black I was used to, the black I had been all my life, nigger is just another insult that shouldn't elicit any more emotional reaction from me than someone calling me a motherfucker. And by then I had been called a motherfucker, fucker, and shithead a few times without having a reaction that was anything close to remarkable. But that late night in St. Cloud, standing between Perkins Restaurant and 1st Street Station Bar and Grill, I remembered what that boy was really saying: that I was nothing short of a slave, an emancipated baboon not fit for freedom, one who could be castrated, have his wife raped in front of him and his children taken away from him, one that White boy could, at one time, violate in the most vicious way and no court would find him guilty of any wrongdoing . . . I jumped and kicked him in the throat!

But then I ran away, because I knew the police station was two short blocks away.

I have been to jail. Stearns County, Benton County, Sherburne County, Hennepin County . . . before I was twenty-five. But check my so-called rap sheet—no guns, no drugs, no theft, no punches. But . . .

1. I did not move fast enough when he told me to move up the sidewalk as I came out of South Beach Night Club in downtown Minneapolis. Disorderly conduct! He tightened the cuffs extra hard for good measure because I was "running my mouth," challenging his authority over me. It took months to lose the numbness in my right thumb.

2. He had been following me since Division, to Ninth Street, left turn onto Michigan Avenue. When I made the right turn from the right lane onto Fifth Street, I was "not close enough to the curb." Driving with a suspended license! Suspended because after losing a semester's worth of credits for nonpayment of tuition, I decided to pay tuition that semester instead of renewing my insurance a few days before I turned into

my parking lot "without signaling." Driving with no insurance! (What was I doing, driving with a suspended license? If I could not afford to buy insurance, maybe I shouldn't have been driving.)

3, Knock, knock! Yes, Officer? Are you guys having a party? Yes, we have few friends over, yes, there is drinking, yes, there is music . . . but it is nothing those girls are not doing right there in the apartment across the parking lot. We are students, doing what college students do on Saturday nights in the comfort of their homes. Why are you here and not there?

If America runs through your veins, you may see the above incidents as either black or white. But . . . if you walk in my shoes . . .

1. Maybe the officer just needed to keep order and peace (in a volatile place like downtown Minneapolis after the clubs). Maybe it was because I was Black.

2. Maybe we both happened to be going the same direction until he saw me making an illegal turn. Maybe he saw a Black guy driving a car and thought I had to be up to no good and it was his duty as a police officer to interrupt whatever illegal activity I was heading toward.

3. Maybe a neighbor, trying to get a peaceful sleep, thought our music was too loud or that we had more than "a few friends" over, and this was not the first time they had called the cops on this house. Maybe it was because they heard "Black" music, knew there was a group of Black people, and certainly a group of Black people, especially young Black people, cannot be a good thing, not for the neighborhood, not for St. Cloud.

Maybe I am just playing the race card. Maybe in America, race is the card I am always dealt.

James Baldwin says, "To be black and conscious in America is to be in a constant state of rage." Even if you are not raging mad, you may be losing your mind. In other words, trouble in mind!

To be Black (and conscious) in America is to always question reality, to constantly hold it to a microscope and analyze its hidden parts. Because nothing is nothing between former slaves and masters, those who hold the gavel and those behind bars.

It is to wonder if that teacher gave you that grade because of the merit of your argument or if he does not like "your kind"—to wonder if your eyes are meeting up with that salesperson for the third time because she finds you attractive or because she finds you suspicious. When I went for an interview for my first off-campus job and did not get hired, was it because I was the only Black candidate, received in an office full of White women? Or was it because I showed up in a tank top fresh from playing basketball? (It was a phone job; I didn't think it was a big deal.) When I applied again a few months later, I got the job. However, when a higher position opened up after a couple of years, it was given to a coworker. But when a project came up later, they remembered my educational background and offered me the project. Only after I delivered above expectations was I promoted. Was that because of my skin color—I had to prove first before being given a chance, while White coworkers got a chance first and an opportunity to prove themselves later? Because the only non-White person in a leadership role at the call center was a Hispanic man in charge of the bilingual group.

It is a heavy burden on the mind to constantly wonder if the wall is indeed bare or if you need only hold a black light to it to see its true color. It gets in the way of living. Who wants that if you can avoid it? I thought I could avoid it. A lot of people in my shoes think they can avoid it.

To be completely honest, I still wish I could avoid it. I wish I could go back to living my life, come in contact with anyone, any institution, and not wonder. Not wonder if it's all in my head, or if indeed my new neighbor, who knew nothing about my former home, was saying "moving is hard, especially when you are moving into a bigger house" because he assumed a Black family moving into a 2,800-square-foot house in Edina has got to be "moving up" like the Jeffersons—or is it just small talk new neighbors make to lighten that awkward moment when they first meet? What did "a guy in the hallways" at my daughter's new (mostly White) school think when he offered my daughter a free bicycle, only for us to show up to collect the bike and find out most of the people collecting free bikes were black and brown children and their families. I got a bike for not only that daughter but my other two children as well. But on the way home, I couldn't shake the nagging feeling that I bet the "guy in the hallway" did not go around offering free bikes to all the kids at the school. Why did he assume that my daughter needed a free bike? It is winter; he certainly did not see other kids riding bikes to school and my daughter walking a lonely path by the side of the road. Why did he assume that the Black kid was likely on free and reduced lunch and her parents could not afford to buy her a used bike?

To be Black in America is to not even see a good deed or accept it for what it is: one human being reaching out to another human being simply because and nothing else. Because between Blacks and Whites, you know often it is not about who you are; rather it is *what* you are: Black and deserving of hate and prejudice, patronization or charity. Maybe it is all in my head. It is all in your head. Until it is not in your head.

Was Barack Obama elected president because he was the most inspiring, most formidable campaigner, most experienced, most gifted with the right leadership qualities . . . or because he was Black, and Americans badly needed to prove to themselves and skeptics that they had turned a new leaf, that we had indeed arrived at Dr. King's dream of a nation where his kids were judged not by the color of their skin but the content of their character? I don't know. I don't think any social scientist can provide a definitive answer. No one can. But many asked this and similar questions. When George W. Bush was elected president, although many believe his last name had everything to do with it, no one wondered if his being White had anything to do with it. When any of the previous forty-three presidents were elected, no one pondered this. When the next White president is elected, no one will talk about whether their race had anything to do with their victory. Had Obama lost, the question would still have been asked.

This is why I struggle with affirmative action. Because though it pries open doors that may otherwise be closed, any Black person who walks through those doors will always have to contend with similar questions, not only from those around and far from him but from his very person. Did I earn it? Am I being held to a different standard—and is that standard higher or lower? This constant wondering is associated not only with anything related to affirmative action but with every facet of being Black in America, especially to be that and successful. It is enough to drive any man insane. To keep your sanity and function properly is testimony to something extraordinarily special about Blacks in this country.

I am trying to say something, but I am not sure I am getting it across clearly. Which may be another way of saying that trying to articulate how it feels to be Black in America is as futile as trying to explain love to someone who's never felt it. It is abstract when you can never imagine your father being choked to death on a New York sidewalk for a fucking cigarette. Nah, scratch that: for trying to breathe life into his hallowed body by asserting his humanity and refusing to be handcuffed by a man who was "always harassing" him. Nah, it's all abstract until that is your husband, who has now left you with six kids standing outside a courthouse where a grand jury just found him guilty of his own murder. It is abstract until you know from experience that the headstone bearing the name "Eric Garner" could easily be your own, your father's, or your son's. Maybe even your mother's. Because when you were eighteen—in Chicago, Minneapolis, or maybe Ferguson, Missouri—you too walked in the middle of a quiet street, and a police officer called you some newfound ways of saying "boy" and "nigger." What did you do? If you were an African, maybe you smiled and respectfully bowed to his demand. (Because you don't know better; you are not familiar with America; the historical memory that is fused in many African Americans' DNA has not permeated your skin yet.) But of course he asked you for identification. When you reached for your wallet, what did he do? He shot you forty-one times. Because he is scared of you, because all his life he has been taught to be aware of the dangerous Black man always out to get him. And now that he has a gun and a license to kill, you best believe he is not taking any chances. Even after he gets you in a holding cell, he could sodomize you just to remind you, 1997 or 1797, Black lives are still subservient to his, and it matters not whether your great-grandfather was a slave in Mississippi, a minister in Haiti, or a prince in Guinea.

I still hesitate to mark "Black" when a form is handed to me. Though I may in fact be the literal manifestation of "African American," I most certainly wouldn't check this if it were a separate option. The label may not be spot-on (labels hardly are), but it is what I have reserved for those Blacks whose ancestors' blood is the water that nourishes the ground America grows on. On the other hand, my ancestors knew nothing of America, not of sun-drenched lifetimes spent in cotton fields; my mother knew nothing about segregated lunch counters, dogs were not set upon my uncles, my great-aunt did not know what it meant to be invited to the massa's quarters. And "the first Black President" makes no sense to my brothers and sisters when you don't add "of America" to it.

But ultimately I check it, the "Black" box. Because in today's reality, it does not matter the blood in my veins; only my barber knows my hair is a bit more kinky than many of his other clients; as long as my skin is dark, I am Black—Black in America and, by extension, many parts of the world. And maybe America has done a number on me—and made me look like my experience— because at a marketplace in Kumasi, northern Ghana, a merchant yelled "Black American!" after me and my family: a Guinean/ Sierra Leonean man with his Ghanaian wife and their American-born children. Yes, we are Black Americans, American-Guineans, American-Ghanaians, American-Africans! Every Black I am is filtered through America. Even the way I love being African, love all things African. Because even the hate I encountered in St. Cloud, especially the hate I encountered in St. Cloud, made me appreciate and love my Black even more.

In an NPR interview, David Oyelowo, the British-Nigerian actor and star of the movie *Selma*, says being Black in America (or any predominantly White country) affects "how you bounce out of bed." If you grow up in a country where you are not a minority, you cannot understand the notion of limit, "that everything on the plate [isn't yours] to eat," something he calls the Sidney Poitier Syndrome. (Poitier was born and raised in the Bahamas.) "I think that if you are brought up in a culture whereby that is not the case, you have a stance of combat, and that invariably means that you are spending more energy trying to burst through than be you."

This is my struggle as a parent. On one hand, it is my hope that my children would consciously mark Black (because they are) and would "bounce out of bed" even though they happen to be in a country that is predominantly White, would work tirelessly, taking for granted that all the food on the plate—as a fair and just reward for their entire labor—is theirs to eat. On the other hand, it is critical that they not be naïve, that they know they are Black in America, a country with a long, heavy history of treating their kind not as full human beings, a country that is still coming to terms with their humanity as wholly and fully exercised as intended by their Creator. When their bodies survive this landmine, I pray that they do not lose their minds trying to balance the two.

BRUTAL

Bao Phi

Bao Phi was born in Saigon and raised in the Phillips neighborhood of South Minneapolis. He has been a performance poet and has struggled to contribute to social justice movements since he was a teenager. He is grateful to the many artists and community organizers who have influenced him.

Growing up as a Vietnamese refugee from war in an American urban neighborhood two blocks from the Native American housing projects does funny things to your already race-addled brain. Okay, so all Asians are forever foreigners, we don't belong here no matter what we do, go back to where you came from, we know all this. But when you also grow up seeing how this country lied and stole from the original people who are *really* from here, it's not just an issue of whether you belong here or not. It also becomes a question of whether you, and anyone else who isn't American Indian, should be here at all.

It was complicated enough, though to deal with my own position. I still do. I grew up in Phillips, which was for the longest time Minnesota's largest, most ethnically diverse, and poorest neighborhood. The library I learned to love, on Franklin Avenue, sat on the block where the American Indian Movement started in the seventies. My youth was spent witnessing bilingual shouting matches in the street, being bullied by Black punk rock kids and Native and Latino metalheads, and getting advice from a former Black Panther and a white Vietnam vet, both of whom wanted to teach me martial arts to defend myself against all of them.

When there was a beef between a crew that called themselves the Naturals and the red beret–wearing Guardian Angels, I sat at home with books or cheap paper sold in packages of two hundred pieces and spent hours sketching with a pen worlds full of dragons, knights, lasers, and spaceships, sometimes trying to replicate things I saw in cartoons or books from the library or *Dragon* magazine back issues I got from Uncle Hugo's on Chicago Avenue.

I was the worst pencil fighter, but they still called me Bruce. I grew older and wore Raiders gear and a white bandana, like a cross between Chuck D and the lead singer of INXS. A kid stood by the graffiti-encrusted pay phones mounted to the brick sides of the 7-11, asking passersby if they wanted to join the Vice Lords. Vietnamese men stood like ghetto kings in smoky dank pool halls, golden money clips glistening on fat green tides of dollar bills. Phillips is where, when I was a little boy, a playground full of kids saw me and began chanting CHINK over and over again in unison, while I walked slowly away, their chant lingering in my ears long after I was out of range. Phillips is where my parents have lived for close to four decades, their house recently ringed by a high fence made of chain link and locked gates. Thunderdome of the ghetto, because a dope boy, chased by cops, ran in one night and ditched his shit. The cops and their police dog spent two days turning over every single rock in my mom's garden.

Inside the doors, my dad told me stories of being on the front lines, picking up pieces of his friend, placing them into a cookie tin so that his family could have the remains. Some of our family and friends were killed—we almost didn't make it ourselves. I was three months old, in the arms of my family, as the shell explosions shook the shelter around us and the many other Vietnamese huddled there. And we were the relatively lucky ones. My father told me that some planes didn't make it off the runway. He watched rockets hit and detonate planes full of Vietnamese people, all of them killed trying to escape. He thought the same would happen to us. Forty years later, he sits at his sewing machine and he tells me he believes that in that moment, when the plane carrying us took off without exploding, all the luck he ever had in life was used up. And that was why we have suffered in America, and why he doesn't want to go back to Vietnam.

I remember arguing with my grandfather because he wouldn't share a can of cheese and noodles he bought with food stamps. Imagine surviving what he did, only to be harassed by me on Twenty-sixth Street in broad daylight in Phillips, for not sharing a can of food. Two of my older brothers joined the U.S. military. Sisters in traditional sword-fighting costumes. My siblings playing instruments and singing in new-wave bands, their impressive coifs aided by cans of Aquanet. I wanted to be Luke Skywalker, the responsible but whiny hero, towel for a cape and my dad's flashlight for a light saber until he demanded it back, not wanting me to waste the batteries. If someone asked me the classic question *where are you really from*, I had no idea how to answer them.

———————

There's another Asian, a girl, smart and sweet as can be. Throughout grade school she will be mercilessly teased because her last name is Ho. When I hear people say shit like *Kids aren't racist*, I have to laugh. Sure they are. All little monsters, waiting to take on final form.

Our classmates were poor white kids, middle-class white kids, and then the white kid who bragged she got forty dollars a week in allowance. Latino/as and Chicano/as. Africans. African Americans. American Indians. Adopted, biracial, multiracial. Southeast Asian refugees, like me. And kids who didn't present gender in a way that made everyone comfortable. I like to joke: sure, I got bullied, but because there were so many different kids around who at any point could be bullied for whatever reason, you came to appreciate the days off. Those times when you counted your lucky stars that the magnifying lens of sudden, ruthless spite wasn't leveled directly at you and your kind during recess.

Except the thing is, I can't remember ever feeling like I had a day off. Even if I wasn't specifically getting chased or threatened or mocked that day, that feeling was always there. It haunted me, closer than my own shadow. My older brothers and sisters, they adapted by becoming tough, aggressive, popular. Beating up kids twice their size in front of everybody. Singing and playing instruments. Being good at sports. I dealt with it by hiding in the Franklin Avenue Library, then running home, or picking a zigzag maze of a way back to the house to avoid the different crews of boys ready to jump me. Because I was a gook, because I was a nerd, because to their eyes I looked like a "fag" or a freak, maybe all of the above. It didn't matter to me—what mattered was that I was faster than them. Then when I got home I dealt with my weakness, my cowardice, by imagining I was someone else, somewhere else. A place with swords made out of lasers, spaceships shaped like wind-thrown hawks, a cape for every hero.

I'm not trying to play a game of poor me, nor do I want to glamorize my own suffering. But one does need to take a cold, hard look at one's past for stories like this because the assumption is Asians don't go through stuff like this in America, right? We quietly go about our lives earning valedictorian status and then go work for Apple, right?

For the most part, those early years sucked. I wasn't just bullied. Hell, my mom and dad were bullied. I learned all the nasty words for my kind early on, from all types and races of kids, sometimes leveled at my parents, sometimes at me. A pretty white girl, in an Asian supermarket, watched her little brother play a video game, and as we little Southeast Asian boys, denied quarters from our parents, quietly gathered to watch him play, she said, "These gooks are surrounding us." The many times my mother or father had gazes fixed on them that clearly read: ignorant. FOB. Gook. Dogeater. Uncivilized. The hatred directed at us was so constant, so thorough, that I hated everything about us that made us different before I even understood how we were different. On the street, sure, and in the lines of the supermarket, at the government offices, too. But also the mainstream papers that claimed we took over Coffman Union and would kill you for looking at one of "our women." The article that suggested we were stealing people's pets and eating them. In sixth grade, a little girl talked about how she saw some family cooking some parrots in their backyard in some huge cauldron, *as if they were witches*, her voice thick with disgust. All those eyes, those African and African

American and Chicano/a and American Indian and white eyes, swung toward me and the two or three other Asians there. I seem to recall insisting my family was not like that. And being relieved when one or two of the kids nodded in approval, then pity. The other Asian kids, I can't remember if they saw me as brave or a fool. I can't remember because all I cared about was myself.

———

By the time the pretty popular blonde tomboy was dating me, I had heard several times that Asian men had small penises. I didn't understand why people cared so much. I was more interested in Dungeons and Dragons, *Star Wars*, anything that allowed me to pretend, no matter how whitewashed, that I was far away from where I actually was. For reasons I can't fathom, she liked me. Me, of all people. We got in trouble in geography class because we joked and laughed together all the time. The teacher thought she was corrupting me (my grade tanked during that time), so he separated our seats. I got a perfect grade on my next quiz, which was identifying all the countries in Southeast Asia on a map, the countries drawn with thick ragged black lines, empty inside their borders.

At the seventh-grade dance a group of white boys, including a friend of mine, watched us dance and said to her, loud enough to hear, *Eeew you're dancing with a gook, you know they only want one thing from white girls.* She rolled her eyes. It wasn't a majority white school. Not even close. Later we met in the Franklin Library and another kid tried to seduce her. I was right there. He was talking dirty to her, promised her he'd do her right. I wasn't a tough kid. I mean, I asked her to meet me at *the library*. My older brother could sometimes make me cry by saying Snoopy was cooler than Garfield. Sensitive, easily provoked, can't fight— bad combo for a refugee kid in the hood. He regaled her with his dirty mouth right in front of me. I felt bad because I could do nothing, didn't know if she wanted me to do anything. I started to wonder how she could choose me. How she could feel something for someone who was nothing. This feeling would remain a part of me forever. Ask my therapist. If you think this is me being possessive and wanting to own her, you're not hearing me. You don't understand, and you won't ever.

It's approximately 1999; I'm in my twenties and protesting *Miss Saigon* for the second time, but unfortunately it won't be the last. We're trained to be respectful, to ask politely if theatergoers would like a free informational booklet with carefully written factoids about Vietnam, refugees, and Asian Americans. Most people ignore us, but some don't. The worst comments come from Asians going to the show. The white people seem to want to avoid discussions on race. The Asians, on the other hand, seem to love to take other Asians down a notch in front of white people. It reaffirms their being. These Asians are often called self-hating, but I think that's a misnomer. They love themselves just fine. It's *other* Asians they hate.

I admit it: I broke the law. I ran a stop sign on a deserted street at night, snow falling in lazy puffs through the arcs of streetlight, contrast harsh there amid low gray-black office buildings butting up against residential streets. I used to walk home from there through the dark train tracks back to Phillips, being on the lookout for people jumping me throughout. Getting pulled over was nothing new—it happened pretty frequently, maybe because Asians had a rep for stealing cars. The officer patted me down. Made me stand outside in the cold while he wrote the ticket. Freezing, I put my hands in my pockets. His hand snaps to his gun. *Get your hands where I can see them*, he says. *You could have a gun.*

It's below zero. He checked me already. But I can only stammer, *I don't have gloves.* He answers, *I don't care.* And he takes his time writing out my ticket.

Asians are more privileged than other people of color, the privileged Asians say, up and down the blogosphere. I see these essays get a lot of play, and when I read them I wonder: how and why would someone assume that their privilege is a reflection of the vast majority of their own people in this country? Especially when they're supposed to be trained to see privilege and systemic injustice: Can they not see their own when they make such claims? On what are they basing these assumptions? Who is their audience? What is behind their dismissal—or in some cases, ignorance—of the struggles that others in the Asian American community face? What does it add to the discussion, the really difficult and necessary discussion, about how differently the races suffer from, and participate in and benefit from, white supremacy, due to a large range of geographical and historical factors?

We know the term "Asian American" is a broad designation that consolidates over thirty different ethnic groups and over a hundred languages, and that if we disaggregate that data, we'll see that the experiences of Asian people in America varies greatly from group to group. With so many languages and experiences, that means various social programs and studies cannot possibly address all Asian American populations, and we must assume that the most underprivileged Asians are marginalized further from Asian American activist movements.

Yet there seems to be a pressure, an insistence, that the Asian American racial experience is funneled through a very myopic lens, where we must acknowledge our privilege or our views on race are not taken seriously. Of course, Asian people in America can and do participate, in some cases willingly, in white supremacy, settler colonialism, anti-Blackness, and anti-immigration. But the positioning of Asian Americans as the least oppressed in dominant discourses on race, and the tacit assumption that we're the *only* people of color who participate in problematic and oppressive behavior against other people of color, puts Asian Americans in a position where the only choices we have are to be in collusion with white supremacy against other people of color or an ally to another community.

Whether villains or allies, what both positions have in common is that they are tangential—we are marginalized, we marginalize our own experience and our own communities. It is tremendously important to work in solidarity with other communities. But we are more than allies. More than villains. We need nuanced, even empathetic, critical examination of our people and our experience.

When I was younger, I embraced the idea of the "exceptional" Asian activist. I wanted to be more down with the cause than other Asians. It made me special. And if I spoke in broad, general terms about my own people, no one would check me. It's just not cool, in any sense, to be associated with Asian people in America. The only time we're not invisible is when we're the enemy. What's cool about that? I wanted to be the Asian that didn't fuck with other Asians. How nice it must be to look at your own family, your own people, and not be reminded of your parents working two or three jobs and getting mugged at the bus stops in the dead of winter, people of all shades throwing *go back to where you come froms*, the police shaking you down for nothing, the newspaper slurs, hiding under the table when your parents fought, fighting most viciously against the people crammed into the same close quarters because you knew each other's languages, each other's families, the various jagged stamps of imperialism marked on your skin like a scar from a polio shot. And that's just my family. What about the ones even less fortunate than me and mine, racially profiled or killed by police then quietly forgotten or deported for making a fuss about it, half of them drowned or raped fleeing their country or—

How nice it must be to be the one Asian down with the others. *Chink but not a chink.* To be a gook but not invisible. *The Chosen One.* To speak on a platform where no one of any consequence will call you out. To be the voice speaking in a language others will hear and remember.

I'm sitting in a spartan community meeting room and a lawyer is telling us the fight for justice for slain Hmong teenager Fong Lee is over. We can't influence the judges because they're appointed for life. They don't have to worry about a voting public. And the judge that decided Jason Andersen, the officer with a history of violence and discrimination against Blacks and Asians, was not guilty of using excessive force when he shot Fong Lee eight times, is a popular judge, and the others won't go against his ruling.

Fong Lee was riding his bike in North Minneapolis with friends when a squad car rolled up to them and gave chase. Apparently riding their bikes together constituted suspicious behavior. The friends got separated, and officer Jason Andersen got out of the squad car and pursued Fong Lee on foot. He shot and killed Lee near a school. A gun, without Lee's fingerprints, DNA, or blood, lay on the wrong side of his body. Video footage from a camera analyzed by experts show that Fong Lee was not holding a gun when fleeing from Officer Andersen. On March 31, 2009, David Hanners of the *Pioneer Press* reported, "the handgun found near a teenager shot and killed by a Minneapolis police officer in 2006 could not have been carried by the teen, new court documents allege: It had last been in possession of police before it was found next to the body of Fong Lee. . . . [T]he gun in question had been recovered earlier after a burglary and turned over to police, who kept it as evidence and had never returned it to its owner."

Fong Lee's family is there, in the meeting room. His mom and dad are handing out water; they are smiling at us, thanking us for what we have tried to have done. I feel less than useless. The type of useless that can only be replaced by a bottomless, tearing rage. I wonder how his beautiful family can be so strong. I wonder how many other Asian families have suffered from police brutality and not reported it—due to fear of men in uniforms with guns, fear of repercussions like deportation, fear of reliving the pain of losing their loved ones as they go through the story again and again.

During the trial, there was a break and the Lee family went to lunch. They came back to a locked courtroom and were told that their son's killer will keep his job and his medal of valor. The judge and the court did not even wait for Fong Lee's family to come back to announce their decision.

———

Asian reality to me was people not speaking English squeezed into tight spaces, never calling the police because of mistrust of uniforms, because of being the alien so of course no one will take your side. Why talk about it? You can't trust anyone, so nothing gets reported. You go home and your parents tell you to learn to fight, they tell you to lie and say you're not Vietnamese. They won't report the bullying—why would they? If you think that this is all paranoia, remember: the U.S. Census, pledged to confidentiality, complied with a request from the U.S. Treasury in 1943 and turned over information to help unjustly incarcerate Japanese Americans during World War II.[1]

Already I feel guilty about talking too much about Fong Lee. About making it "my cause." I'm not Hmong. I did not suffer the way his family did. I was not even the hardest-working member of the activist group involved in the case. But I was there. And the Asian American activists writing these op-eds who say Asians don't suffer from racial profiling and police brutality were not there.

———

Jason Chu creates a video called "They Won't Shoot Me." While the piece is meant to be an exploration of his own privilege, it is nonetheless troubling in that viewers at large, who may already believe Asian Americans suffer less than other people of color and indigenous people, may infer that Asian Americans don't suffer from police brutality—and Fong Lee, Chonburi Xiong, Michael Cho, Kao Kuan Chung, and Cau Thi Bich Tran are just

———

[1] Haya L. Nasser, "Papers Show Census Role in WWII Camps," *USA Today*, March 30, 2007, usatoday30.usatoday.com/news/nation/2007-03-30-census-role_N.htm.

the more well-known cases that contradict that idea. Nineteen-month-old Bounkham "Bou Bou" Phonesavanh was disfigured when a SWAT team threw a flashbang grenade into his crib in a botched drug raid—no Asian American spoken word poems and videos are popping up on my newsfeed about this. In an article in the *Huffington Post*, Pulitzer Prize–winning journalist Jose Antonio Vargas claims, "No one is being stopped by the police for driving while Asian." Mr. Vargas is an accomplished, well-respected thinker who has done much to bring discussions of race and power to the forefront in mainstream journalism. It's disappointing that he would be so reckless in dismissing racial profiling that does affect Asian American people.

Perhaps it is unfair to expect Asian American arts activists and public intellectuals like Chu and Vargas to be conscious of or knowledgeable about Asians being racially profiled when so much of my own knowledge of these cases is personal and anecdotal. My Asian friends and I were pulled over repeatedly under suspicion that we were car thieves or participating in illegal street-racing activities. I was stopped once for no reason, and the officer asked me if I stole my car, even though I had a license and registration. Other Asian women and men have told me stories about being racially profiled, and in some cases abused, by police officers and authority figures. Yet the prevailing notion is that Asian Americans don't suffer from racial profiling, police brutality, or state-sanctioned violence. But if Asian Americans don't call attention to these issues, who will?

———

In the Twin Cities alone, the corrupt police Gang Strike Force was known to racially profile Black, Latino, Native American, and Southeast Asian—especially Hmong—men. In 2003, Duy Ngo, a Vietnamese undercover police officer with the Minnesota Gang Strike Force, was shot by an on-duty white police officer, Charles Storlie, with an illegal firearm while Duy was lying on the ground. Ngo had been shot by an unidentified suspect and had called for help. According to Ngo's account, the squad car rolled up to him with its lights turned off as he lay prone, and the officers failed to announce their presence—all against regulation. Officer Storlie then shot several bursts at Duy with a non-regulation MP5 submachine gun, shattering his left forearm, leg, and groin, permanently disabling him.

Apparently, the officer who shot Ngo thought he was an Asian gang member. Duy was shocked to find that the police force he was so loyal to quickly turned on him. Rumors spread that Duy was racist or at fault, that he had shot himself to avoid military service, and that it was his fault for working solo and breaking departmental rules. The white officer who shot him with an illegal firearm was put on paid leave for three days. No criminal charges were filed against that officer, and an internal affairs investigation found no policy or procedural violations. Incidentally, this was the same officer who had shot a fifteen-year-old boy holding a BB gun a few years before.

After years of struggling with health issues brought on by the shooting, Duy Ngo sued the department and the city to clear his name. He won a $4.5 million settlement in 2007. It "was never about the money," Ngo commented at the time. "It was about justice." For those cynical readers who may be scoffing, know that the injuries Ngo sustained in that shooting led to him being permanently disabled and in pain for the rest of his life. Three years after winning the settlement, Ngo died in 2010 via a self-inflicted gunshot wound to the head.

Jason Andersen, the officer who shot and killed Fong Lee, was also part of this Gang Strike Force.

How many more cases like these stay invisible because our own people can't figure out how to fit them into their ideas of racial hierarchies? Make no mistake: the horrendous police brutality epidemic against Black bodies and Native bodies is reprehensible and inhumane. This is not a "me too" plea that flattens the ways different non-white people suffer from racism in this country. I would assert that educating ourselves and allies about the police brutality cases that have affected Asian American communities does not take away from the discourse; it strengthens it, and potentially allows us to reach and involve Asian American communities who may not have the same access to discourse and frameworks on race and social justice organizing that those of us who are college educated and English speaking, myself included, do.

And to be clear, this is not to say we should talk about these often-ignored cases of police brutality against Asian Americans at the expense of the Black and Native struggle, nor to excuse our participation in white supremacy. It is a suggestion that we should do all of the above.

I'm not part of Fong Lee's family or Ngo's, yet I feel what it means to be a part of that gravity, that pull, that collision of hurt and tragedy. And Asian American history, particularly our history of struggle, is obfuscated and difficult to access, even for us. If we don't keep this ignored history, if we don't empathize with our people, who will? *Asians don't suffer from police brutality; therefore these incidents don't exist.*

———

Is it just me? Am I as bad as a white person who claims white people also suffer from discrimination?

Let's do some digging. American Community Survey data shows that Southeast Asian Americans, particularly Hmong and Khmer, suffer from higher poverty rates than the national averages. Family income rates for Southeast Asians are well below the national average, and when we look at individual median incomes Asians overall still make less than whites. The statistics: on average, 12.4 percent of U.S. citizens live below the poverty line; it's 12.4 percent for Asian Americans. Poverty rate for Hmong: 37.8 percent; Cambodian: 29.3 percent; Laotian: 18.5 percent; Vietnamese: 16.6 percent.[2]

Immigration policies in the United States favor highly skilled, highly educated Asians: the brain drain from India and China

———

[2] Initiative on Asian Americans and Pacific Islanders, "Critical Issues Facing Asian Americans and Pacific Islanders," www.whitehouse.gov/administration/eop/aapi/ data/critical-issues.

received the lion's share, 71.6 percent, of H1-B visas.[3] Combining
these relatively privileged Asian immigrants with refugees from
Southeast Asia, poorer and undocumented Asians, and sometimes Pacific Islanders who also suffer from a legacy of settler
colonialism and land and resource theft, obscures the bigger picture of Asian struggle.[4] The incarceration rate of Asian Americans
and Pacific Islanders quadrupled from 2000 to 2010; with disaggregated data, Samoans and Vietnamese have the highest rate of
arrest of any ethnic group in San Francisco.[5]

The numbers of Asians in higher education in the United
States is often cited as an indicator of Asian success. However,
often those numbers are conflated by overseas Asian students,
part of the brain drain from their homelands, whose experience
and relative privilege is different from that of Asian Americans.
When the data is disaggregated, only 17 percent of Pacific Islanders, 14 percent of Cambodians, 13 percent of Laotians, 26 percent
of Vietnamese, and 13 percent of Hmong people in the United
States have bachelor's degrees.[6]

Southeast Asians have low graduation rates from high school,
nationally, and, broken down into respective groups, the high
school drop-out rate among Southeast Asian Americans is staggering: 40 percent of Hmong, 38 percent of Laotian, and 35 percent of Cambodian populations do not complete high school. This
suggests that many Southeast Asians either cannot successfully

---

[3] Marcus Chan, "Biggest Brain Drains: India Gets Nearly Two-Thirds of U.S. H1-
Bs," *Global Tech*, August 20, 2013, www.bloomberg.com/news/2013-08-20/india-
nabs-nearly-two-thirds-of-u-s-h-1b-visas.html.

[4] Sharon H. Chang, "The Growing Poverty Crisis that Everyone Is Ignoring," *Think
Progress*, September 26, 2015, thinkprogress.org/immigration/2015/09/26/3705261/
asian-american-poverty/.

[5] Randall, "Incarceration of Asian Americans and Pacific Islanders Increasing
at Rapid Rate," *AsAmNews*, October 23, 2015, www.asamnews.com/2015/10/23/
incarceration-of-asian-americans-pacific-islanders-increasing-at-rapid-rate/.

[6] Sahra Vang Nguyen, "The Truth About 'The Asian Advantage' and 'Model Minority
Myth,'" *Medium*, October 12, 2015, medium.com/@oneouncegold/the-truth-about-
the-asian-advantage-and-model-minority-myth-fbd3bb210b3c#.4wph9sdvz.

navigate the American educational system or the education system is failing them—or both.[7]

And of note: even if we are to take the simplistic look that Asian bodies, regardless of their sociopolitical/historical reasons for being in this country, are overrepresented in the U.S. higher education system, only seventy schools out of the roughly three thousand four-year institutions in the United States offer classes on Asian American Studies. Which suggests that even if Asian Americans get racialized and radicalized during their higher education, chances are it's not with an Asian American lens.[8]

Post 9/11, Arabs and South Asians and anyone "presenting" as Muslim faced state-sanctioned violence as well as, obviously, good old-fashioned racist mainstream violence on the street.[9] The horrific murders of Deah Shaddy Barakat, Yusor Mohammad Abu-Salha, Razan Mohammad Abu-Salha, and Navroze Mody and the shooting at Oak Creek, while not committed by police, suggest a vigilante violence informed by Orientalism, making Sikhs and Muslims into enemy alien "others." For state-sanctioned violence informed by Orientalism, one can consider the files on Guantanamo, which were released to seemingly very little fanfare.[10] And of course, Jianqing "Jessica" Klyzek, Chonburi Xiong, Fong Lee, Cao Thi Bich Tran, Kang Wong, Michael Cho, Jason Yang, Yong Xin Huang, Kao Kuan Chung, Phung Ho—these are only the most well-known cases of police brutality.

---

[7] Initiative on Asian Americans and Pacific Islanders, "Critical Issues."

[8] Sylvia Regan, "It's About Time You Took an Asian American Studies Class," Advancing Justice/AAJC, *Medium*, October 7, 2015, medium.com/advancing-justice-aajc/it-s-about-time-you-took-an-asian-american-studies-class-4c83d6e3f29.

[9] Christopher Ingraham, "Anti-Muslim Hate Crimes Are Still Five Times More Common Today than Before 9/11," Wonkblog, *Washington Post*, February 11, 2015, www.washingtonpost.com/news/wonkblog/wp/2015/02/11/anti-muslim-hate-crimes-are-still-five-times-more-common-today-than-before-911/.

[10] Charlie Savage, William Glaberson, and Andrew W. Lehren, "Classified Files Offer New Insights into Detainees," The Guantánamo Files, *New York Times*, April 24, 2011, www.nytimes.com/2011/04/25/world/guantanamo-files-lives-in-an-american-limbo.html.

And really, it doesn't take that much, not even access to the Internet, to realize that the populations of Asian Americans least likely to get into blog and think piece slugfests on the Internet are the least privileged of us. The ones who have no social service workers, activists, or lobbyists who speak their dialect. Who may be undocumented. The ones other Asians wonder about: *where are they from?*

––––––––––––

My daughter's daycare is five minutes from my apartment. One day, we are late and, seeing no one, I roll through a stop sign. The police materialize out of nowhere, and they pull me over, just around the corner from daycare. It's 9:35 AM, a bright and sunny day. One police officer is standing on the curb, on the passenger side, just a few feet behind where my daughter is raised on her car seat. He has his hand on his gun. Ready to draw. I can see him in the mirror. The other officer also has his hand on his gun when he asks me for my license and registration. Later, a fellow Asian American upon hearing my story will insist it wasn't racial, that all police have a hand on their guns when stopping someone. I know this is not true because my white friends say this has not happened to them. I wonder what the officers thought I could possibly be doing, in broad daylight, in the morning, with my four-year-old daughter in the booster seat, that would warrant them needing their guns.

Her classmates are Black, white, Latino, American Indian. Dropping her off, I was overwhelmed. Everyone—the teachers, her classmates, her teacher's teenage son—could be Mike Brown. Or Lili Wang, Fong Lee, CeCe McDonald, L.M.J., Matthew Shepard, Luis Ramirez, and the list goes on. I'm not saying all of those lives and stories are the same—I'm saying I saw this rainbow of kids, and instead of being encouraged, I got scared in a different way for each one of them. I couldn't shake a panicked feeling that I wanted to be there to put my arms around them and shield them all—but I couldn't. No one could.

Like my daughter's friends, mine were also from all over. All races, all of that. But it didn't save me, and it didn't save them.

———————

The other day I saw a group of kids at a restaurant playing Magic: The Gathering. It was five boys. They were a mix of Hmong, Chicano, and South Asian. They were really into their nerd-ass game, but they weren't being disruptive. They were completely present with one another, throwing down, enjoying the competition, sitting in a circle so close their elbows touched. You wouldn't be able to fit at that table even if they invited you. Such a sight isn't really rare anymore. But I loved them just the same. They didn't care what anyone thought of them. They were crew. They argued the game's rules among themselves; they set limits to the magic. They were fearless.

SAY WHAT?

Carolyn Holbrook

Carolyn Holbrook, recipient of a Minnesota State Arts Board Artist Initiative grant and the Minnesota Book Awards' Kay Sexton Award, is the author of *Ordinary People, Extraordinary Journeys* and the founder of SASE: The Write Place (now merged with Intermedia Arts). She dedicates this piece to her son, Julian Montgomery.

For years, I have heard compliments about my voice. People who participate in my journaling workshops frequently describe my voice as soothing, and they tell me it makes them feel safe enough to reveal things they hadn't shared before. My college students often say my voice is warm yet authoritative. They tell me it makes them listen, even when I'm saying something that doesn't have much substance. Back in the eighties my friend Carter called me "E. F. Holbrook," comparing my voice to the popular commercials about the E. F. Hutton brokerage firm. "When E. F. Hutton speaks, people listen," the voiceover proclaimed. I laughed, but clearly, Carter heard what my students hear. And let's not forget the men who said my voice had put a spell on them. One of them joked that I could make a lot of money doing phone sex.

My children hear my voice in ways others are not privy to: the gentle tones, when they were little, that convinced them that the silly songs I sang out of tune would heal their owies; the shrill, scratchy tone that came out nearly unbidden when my anger exploded like thunder when they were teenagers; the authoritarian voice that left no doubt that I meant it when I said "If y'all don't get yo nappy heads up in here, I'm gonna (fill in the blank)"; the icy tones that said they had disappointed me; the calm, reassuring voice they hear as adults when they're second-guessing themselves and need reassurance—and at those times when, as one of my daughters puts it, "Mom, I need you to talk me down off of a cliff."

I have often wondered if I could earn extra income doing television and radio commercials, or narrating videos and audiobooks. Maybe I could be one of the first women to voice movie trailers. In 2006, after I completed a merger that blended the literary arts organization I founded with another arts organization, I decided to find out. I had been using my voice to lead literary programs and to teach creative writing, composition, and journal writing for a number of years, and I thought this might be a good time to expand my world. My voice had already provided me with small opportunities: I had narrated a couple of short films for a neighbor.

Conversations with acquaintances who do this kind of work, coupled with a Google search, revealed that there are a good number of talent agencies in the Twin Cities, some that offer training in voice acting. When a friend recommended her high school buddy's father, an actor/teacher/talent agent, I decided to give him a call. I liked the way he described his workshops, and the price was definitely right. He said he was offering a three-weekend workshop for beginners that would start the following week, so I told him to sign me up.

The instructor's studio was in the basement of his home, and he had instructed me to enter through the back door. My son, Julian, who composes and produces urban hip-hop gospel music, also has a state-of-the-art studio in his basement, and he assured me that this was not unusual. I arrived late the first day, the usual for me, and I was a little nervous, expecting to be the only dark person in the room, also the usual. I drove through the middle-class suburban neighborhood slowly and looked at the little white, beige, and light blue bungalows, hoping not to attract any attention. I parked in front of the man's house and walked around to the back with my head up and shoulders back, trying not to look out of place in case any of his neighbors were watching. I hesitated for a moment when I reached the back door, and when I didn't hear any sirens, I assumed that no one had called

911 to report a strange black woman lurking around the house. Then I opened the door and started gingerly down the stairs, hands sweating as I held on to the railing and took in the musty basement smell. When I reached the bottom of the stairs and turned into the room where the class was being held, I was relieved by the warm welcome I received from the instructor and the other students, all of them white, as I had expected. A thirty-ish blonde woman dressed in denim cutoffs and a T-shirt flashed a bright smile and patted the empty seat next to her on the old sofa where she sat in the dimly lit room.

Just like Julian's basement studio, this one was equipped with professional microphones, mic stands, music stands, sound equipment, and a computer. Cables were neatly taped to the worn shag carpet, presumably to prevent injuries to clumsy people like me who might trip over them.

I could tell right away that the workshop was going to be well worth the time, energy, and money I had expended to be there. The man clearly knew his stuff. The other participants were friendly and, like me, eager to find out if their voices had the potential to be successful in this type of work. The man's teaching style was an effective blend of lecture and demonstration. He invited students to ask questions whenever they came up, and he took the time to give thorough responses. And though his personality was a bit curmudgeonly, his occasional smile, a brief, flickering twinkle that flashed through the lenses of his horn-rimmed glasses rather than from upturned lips, showed that he enjoyed sharing his knowledge.

Much of the workshop time was spent with students taking turns at the mic reading from scripts the instructor had placed on a music stand and receiving his feedback on the power, resonance, and overall quality of our voices. Indeed, I tripped over the cables on the floor when it was my turn. And then, in keeping with my innate clumsiness, I spilled the papers onto the floor while rifling through them to decide what to read. When I picked them up, a script for a Progresso soup commercial was on top. I decided to read that one and save myself any further embarrassment.

I don't remember the exact words, but the script went something like this: "We love your Weight Watchers–endorsed soups. My husband looks the way he did twenty years ago."

The teacher instructed me to read it again several times, each time giving me tips on how to make my voice more effective.

"Breathe from your diaphragm," he ordered. Then, "Say it like you mean it. Remember how your husband looked twenty years ago!" His voice was an interesting blend of Marlon Brando Godfather raspiness tinged with a touch of gentle matter-of-factness, a voice that perfectly matched his personality. My smiling classmates applauded and I felt relieved when he finally declared, "There. Now I believe you. Now I wanna buy that soup."

Three weekends later, when the workshop was over, I felt pretty confident that what I had been hearing all those years was true, that indeed I had the potential to be a voice actor. My next step would be to make a recording of my voice and send it off to talent agencies. My son agreed to make my CD and to record his own voice as well since he, too, had an interest in this work.

I spent the next few weeks standing in front of my bathroom mirror reading ad copy, stories, poems, and newspaper articles aloud, practicing breathing from my diaphragm and projecting my voice, and imitating voices I heard on commercials. I smiled when Julian called one day and asked, "Mom, are you ready yet?" Though he was in his thirties, the call took me back to his childhood, reminding me of every small child's query: "Are we there yet?"

———————

The instructor had promised to keep us informed about opportunities and auditions whenever they came up, and true to his word, he started sending frequent e-mails. One of them, a commercial for a wet mop, caught my attention. I responded with an e-mail expressing my interest and letting him know that I hadn't yet recorded my CD. He said not to worry: he would be doing the auditions himself, over the phone. I wouldn't need to read the copy the company would be using for the commercial, he said, because at this point, they were simply looking for the right voice. I could choose what I would read.

We scheduled the audition for the following week, and I intensified my bathroom mirror performances, happy with my new ability to breathe from my diaphragm and allow my naturally soft voice to project and exude more power. I read passages from Isabel Allende's memoir *Paula*, about the daughter she lost to a horrific illness. I've always been fascinated with her ability to seamlessly weave the political climate she left behind in her native Chile with whatever story she is telling in her novels and memoirs. I read print ads that attracted me either because they were great ads or because they were so sexist that they disgusted me, in the latter case hoping to achieve a voice that warned, "Ladies if you buy the line of crap this company is selling, you will be demeaning yourself and the rest of womanhood." And I read poems and song lyrics until, standing before the mirror, projecting my voice fully, I decided what to read: the great Nikki Giovanni's "Ego Tripping (there may be a reason why)" always makes me stand up straighter, confident in my own strength, power, and beauty, despite the way America portrays me and my sisters, daughters, and granddaughters.

The night before the audition I kept waking up and looking at the clock for fear that I would oversleep and miss it, even though the audition wasn't until 10:00 and I never sleep past 6:00. I got up a couple times and practiced. Then, for the entire hour before the appointed time, I stood in front of the desk in my home office watching the Mississippi River flow past my window while I practiced breathing properly and projecting my voice, all the while praying that my fatigue wouldn't come through.

Finally, it was 10:00. I took a deep breath, picked up the phone, and dialed the instructor's number. He greeted me warmly and explained his process for doing phone auditions, saying that he would record my voice using equipment that would make me sound like I was live in his studio. He told me to read as though I was standing in front of one of his microphones, took me through a brief sound check, and then said he would cue me when it was time to begin. I took another deep breath and, on his cue, began.

"I was born in the congo," I read, feeling pride and power in my voice.[1]

> I walked to the fertile crescent and built the sphinx
> I designed a pyramid so tough that a star
> > that only glows every one hundred years falls
> > into the center giving divine perfect light
> I am bad

I took another breath and continued:

> I sat on the throne
> > drinking nectar with allah
> I got hot and sent an ice age to europe
> > to cool my thirst
> My oldest daughter is nefertiti
> > the tears from my birth pains
> > created the nile
> I am a . . .

"Carolyn," the man interrupted. I thought I heard some urgency in his voice, but I ignored it and kept reading.

> . . . beautiful woman.

"Carolyn," he repeated, a little louder and with authority. I stopped reading. "Carolyn," he repeated a third time. "Take the black out of it."

Did I hear him right?

---

[1] From Nikki Giovanni, *The Collected Poetry of Nikki Giovanni: 1968–1998* (New York: Harper Perennial Modern Classics, 2007). Reprinted with permission.

"Take the black out of it," he repeated. Yes, I had heard him right.

"Take. The. Black. Out of it!" he exclaimed a third time.

―――――――

I stood in a heavy silence, my heart turning to stone from the weight of his words. I pictured the tall, skinny man sitting at his work station wearing the wrinkled white shirt, unbuttoned at the neck, that he had worn to all three of the workshop sessions, and in my mind, I repeated the encouraging words he had uttered while critiquing me in his basement studio. I wanted to ask him, "Didn't you notice the black in my voice when I read the scripts on your music stand?"

I wonder what his response would have been if I had asked him some of the questions that ran through my mind. What if I had asked him to give me a reason why I should take the black out of my voice. "There may be a reason," Nikki Giovanni said. I'm guessing he would have stammered a bit and then replied that the company he was representing wanted a traditional voice (need I state the obvious: that "traditional" translates as white?). I wonder if he would have had the guts to tell me that the company didn't think the American public was ready for the multitude of voices that make up this nation today. I seriously doubt it. Instead, when I started reading, he had uttered the first words that came to his mind, the words that meant what he truly intended—uncensored, not coated with the processed sugar known as *Minnesota Nice*.

I wish I had thought to ask him if he would be willing to take the Irish out of his voice, to negate his identity, but when I was finally able to speak, I couldn't find words. Truth is, the poem I read could have been written by any Black poet, past or present: Gwendolyn Brooks, Lucille Clifton, Audre Lorde, Maya Angelou, or June Jordan. She could have been a contemporary poet—maybe Natasha Trethewey, Elizabeth Alexander, Nikky Finney, or Rita Dove. She could have been a local poet—Mary Moore Easter, Tish Jones, Kyra Crawford-Calvert, or Sherrie

Fernandez-Williams. Or it could have been a male poet. It didn't matter who the poet was: the man's reaction would have been the same. He probably would have seen any poem that spoke to strength or equality, one that offered a call for my people to rise up against the odds and be inspired to feel pride in who we are, as a threat to his power.

While I stood at my window searching for words, I remembered a powerful scene from *Roots*, the iconic 1977 television miniseries. Every detail was clear.

A crowd of slaves on a plantation in Annapolis, Maryland, watched in horror as a slave who had run away was captured and brought in for public punishment. Three white men on horses ordered two slave men to spread the younger man's arms out and bind his wrists to each end of an iron bar. They then pulled the bar up with a rope and fit it into notches carved into two wooden posts that they had pounded into the ground. The young man screamed words in an African language, and everyone in the crowd understood he was pleading for help from whatever gods he believed in.

One of the white men climbed off of his horse, handed a long leather whip to one of the slaves, James, who had bound the runaway.

"Say your name!" the overseer commanded in a thick Irish accent, and then he repeated the words. Each command was followed by more lashes from the whip and screams that made those in the crowd wonder how much life the boy had left in his bones.

"My name is Kunta . . . Kunta Kinte," the young man replied in broken English, desperation threading through every syllable.

More lashes. "Your name is Toby," the overseer insisted.

"My name is Kunta Kinte," the young slave repeated, refusing to give in.

"When the master gives you something, you take it. He gave you the name Toby. It's a nice name, and it's gonna be yours till the day ye die." The man's tone was shockingly nonchalant.

"I . . . am . . . Kunta . . . Kinte," gasped the young man, trying with everything he had left to hold on to his identity.

"I want to hear you say your name. Your name is Toby," said the overseer and gestured for James to deliver more lashes.

Finally, when the young man had no reserves left, he said in a weak voice, "My . . . my name is Toby."

"Say it louder so they can all hear ye," said the man, pointing dismissively at the onlooking crowd of slaves.

"My name . . . my name . . . is Toby," gasped the young man.

"Aye," said the overseer. "That's a good nigger."

The women in their gunnysack dresses, their heads wrapped to hide their kinky hair, and the men in torn shirts and raggedy pants, all stared at the young man, their faces full of the grief of knowing that another one of them had had the black beaten out of his voice.

———————

"Carolyn. Carolyn. Are you there, Carolyn?"

"No," I whispered. I hung up the phone, then called my son and told him I wouldn't be making the voice CD for a while. "I don't think I'm ready yet."

RED, WHITE, AND BLANK

Heid E. Erdrich

Heid E. Erdrich is Ojibwe, enrolled at Turtle Mountain. She is author of four collections of poetry and co-editor of *Sister Nations: Native American Writers on Community*. Her most recent book is *Original Local: Indigenous Foods, Stories, and Recipes from the Upper Midwest*. She mentors MFA students at Augsburg College.

I've been lying about my race my whole life. I've never lied about my race.

My face lies about my race, my whiteness defies me and defines me. My birth record asks *Race of Mother? Race of Father?* Leaves for my race a blank, a fill-in-the blankness of someone's choosing. Did my *American Indian* mother choose my race or my *Caucasian* father? Did a nurse or clerk choose, usually? And how would she decide? My siblings' birth records might say something other, I do not know.

> Whiteness
> my own blank sign
> here here here
> and here

> Race
> line lines signs
> here here here
> and here

Here's where I stop and start. Here's where I write what I want to say, over and over and over. Here in the paragraph break between what I do not know above and what I know below. Here's where I've drafted nearly everything that follows. I wrote and cut and pasted it elsewhere. There were deletions, too, and they are still here for you to sense, but not to see.

———

Events in 2014 put a national focus on race and rage. So many people I knew were righteously outraged and enraged, then rage fatigued, outrage addicted, and finally displacing rage or cyber-raging. I tried to write how, because I look white, that rage undid me, hit me, made me face my face. Then I wrote past rage and where it got or did not get me. I wrote until I knew what I did not know. And here is where I am beyond deletion.

Blank.

———

There should be a long blank space between what I do not know and what I know. This space should be long as my life. This space should not be white, but be a blankness filled with energy that attracts and repels like the force field we feel when holding two magnets together. But it should also be less about *two things* and more of a sense of *many*. No "walking in two worlds" for me. Less a binary and division. A not-yet-reflecting mirror. A gray field not yet filled. In a society where race often means Black and white, who I am must mean invisible.

Blank, but not white.

I want to make room as I write for a sense of what is not visible. There should be an open space, a tension and resting moment at once. A place where my audience—you who are reading—can be like me and still un-like me enough to let me explain how I experience race without think-

ing I am working out my identity. I am not working out my identity. I know and have always known who I am. My being requires the making of new space. Some kind of prism of resistance and pull. That is where I live, and it is impossible to put it here, even though it is here, this space, this palpable presence between what I can tell you and what you can't know, between what I know and what I can't know.

——————

What I do know: If I were to say that I am white, I'd be lying.

Long ago such things bothered me. As a young person I found others (of all races) demanded I define my identity. Five other people who were exactly my mix had done this before me. One of my sisters answered, *I would be lying if I didn't say I'm Indian.* What question I asked was this: What did she say when people asked if she was white? Yes, people ask one another if they are white or if they are Indian. And we are expected to answer. And we'd be lying if we didn't. Didn't what? Didn't say. Say what? What is true.

I want room again already. A little space here to let you sense what is not visible. Sense the fact of the Indigenous person.

——————

Most people would not know the Indigenous person on the street because we do not often look like the centuries-old image that myth and media teach the world to expect. Not looking like that Woodland Maiden or Plains Warrior leaves a gap where most of us live and that gap makes us invisible. So we often have to say, have to explain, every last brown or beige one of us, that we are Indian.

But now I do not even know I am that, anymore. That *Indian.* That word is an umbrella handed to us by colonizers. Named by that force that makes possible all *racial tension,* all erasure and absenting, all the gaps, all exclusiveness and owning. To be *Indian* in "a nation of immigrants" erases over five hundred nations' names for themselves and relates us to a distant continent. It does not say we are still here. It cannot explain what the word means to us, and it means different things to different Indians. I grew up sheltered under the word *Indian*, it made me feel at home, if not safe. Now, less and less that name means who we are or who I am. For sure *Indian* means who I've been and who we've been. *American Indian* is the compromise that eases many people, makes them proud. For a long time I was comfortable with *Native American* because at least the continent and country were correct. I'm leaning more toward *Indigenous* these days. Our cultures and histories are tied inextricably to these lands, and they arose here, Indigenously. To me, *Indigenous* makes sense. It makes others mad. They want us to settle and be one thing they know. To check one box. Until that box says *human*, I'll be lying when I check it. We will all be lying. We will all be telling the truth. Impossible.

Some folks leave the box blank. Blank for me would be a lie.

My tribe and legal status make me Chippewa, Ojibwe, Anishinaabe. Even then it's hard to claim *Chippewa*, the name being the old and wrong way that Europeans (then Americans, then we too) used to say Ojibwe. *Anishinaabe*, being how we speak of ourselves, seems it should be used among ourselves and extend to Potawatomi and Odawa folks who call themselves the same. When I came to live in Minnesota, the home of most Ojibwe south of Canada, it made sense I'd say I am Ojibwe. Still, officially, as in some office somewhere states, I am Chippewa. Officially, as in the card in my wallet states, I am Chippewa. A tribal member. Numbered and enrolled at the Turtle Mountain Reservation in North Dakota. I have a tribe and, by extension, relationship to specific people—we are like cousins, all of us—and this relates me to other tribes, to all the people who arose here in this hemisphere. It is all about relationship.

Being related centered my life. Standing in relationship came as conscious lesson from my mother. It started with my six siblings, my grandparents, uncles, aunts, cousins. We noted relatedness with one another, established it when greeting, used our kinship terms. Relatedness extended to my one thousand cousins and their kin. I would never lie about who I am to my relatives. I would never lie about my relatives by denying them. In Minnesota I began to learn Ojibwemowin, our language. Anishinaabe say *Indinawemaaganidog: all my relations. We are all related.*

My children are my closest relatives. My self split into two with their father there, too. They are whole to me. They are mine and should be Ojibwe. But we count blood in a messed up mathematics decreed by government. This is how we control and diminish our tribal rolls. My children cannot be enrolled. Are my children white? I will never think so, but I do not know.

What I do know: Miscegenation taboos were enshrined in law books in most states when my parents married. Or let me say more plainly: because my father was white and my mother American Indian, they could have been denied the right to marry. I was three years old when a court case, one that gave us Loving Day, was decided in 1967. To be legal is to exist in this country. Loving made us real.

The laws used words like "colored" or "octoroon," but Indigenous people are not exactly People of Color. We may be generally brown (we can be and are Black), but we are not immigrants, forced or otherwise, and we do not have a uniform racial identity. We are, like more and more Americans, distinct groups who claim our own particular mix depending upon our lands and borders because we are, foremost, political entities. Nations. Nations built in bodies.

And here's yet another contradiction: Many of my mother's people referred to themselves as *mixed-blood*. So very Harry Potter, I know, so *mudblood*. For a long time *mixed-blood* was a comfortable term for me. Eventually it disturbed my sense of being whole and now I rarely use it. I did not teach the term to my children to use for themselves, although it is part of their history. I respect what it once meant. *Mixed-blood* made sense to my ancestors, some of whom had a white parent or grandparent and some of whom used the term to mean Indigenous people who adopted some white ways of living, like farming or going to church or using English. The term was also a tool for the government to shrink the number of people they owed, under treaties.

Mixed-blood status was not determined by DNA test, but was a term that could be bestowed on Indigenous people just because they had chairs in their homes. After that? Fewer in the tribe, more land to grab. I grew up hearing *mixed-blood*, and to me it meant a kind of sub-tribe of Anishinaabe. No one talked about being mixed as being white.

Walking down the street, I am white to most folks. Often, the ones who walk with me, my relatives, are not. White. Whether I want it or not, I wear my whiteness like a key fob. Doors open for me. I've held doors open for relatives. I am being figurative, but literally my door holding is also true. The fact that I've had to do that? That's not nice. Not nice for me knowing and holding privilege and resisting it at once—and knowing I have no choice. Not nice for my relatives—my being contrasting the unfair treatment of their own. This is reality, and it does not matter that skin privilege is as unbidden as it is unearned.

And here I want to make another space where I can to write to those like me who understand what it means to look, but not be, white. Or those whose relatives wear whiteness and its ease every day. Some things we cannot choose. It is impossible to live beyond our embodied truth. Our sweet skins hold our spirits in—all of us—and we must love ourselves. But whiteness is never as blank as it can look.

It is a sweet Minnesota spring evening, and another child of a Black parent is dead. Black Lives Matter organizes a rally. This is Minnesota and, of those gathered at Gold Medal Park, as many seem white as are Black. There are many, many couples with children who are both white and not. White. Speeches start. Sage smoke drifts over the crowd, and we take to the streets. We fall in near other Indigenous folks—some I recognize but don't know by name. Near us is a small group of writers I know: Black, white, Asian. On their shoulders small children ride, floating black balloons on strings. This is Minnesota, and the crowd seems unafraid, almost celebratory, a bit tame. The police keep their distance this time.

At some point the organizers use a bullhorn to ask the people of color to come to the front of the line. They ask for Black and brown bodies to head the march. No one near me cuts through the crowd. A group of Black teenagers next to me tease a much less dark boy that they'll go ahead and he can stay and pass—he says he never would. They all hang back. None of the people of color near me leave their white family members to join those at the front. I glance at my children and husband, who do not seem to notice the moment when I decide not to go.

At dinner after the march my teenage son asks for the salt. I remind him not to use too much. His little sister asks why salt is bad. My son says, "It is bad because it is white, just like our privilege." And we laugh.

I need space again. Blank force. A lightless mirror you can stare into. So here I make a room for you to sense what is not visible.

—————

When we were teens the rumor went around that if you stare at a mirror in the dark long enough you can sense someone there and soon Crazy Horse's ghost would appear. It never happened to anyone I knew, but we tried it anyhow. Something like that should be happening now.

Take a moment to sense something not visible in all that has happened from Ferguson to Baltimore. It's a sense of deeper force behind our national problems with race, our *Minneapolis Miracle* that leaves out African American and African immigrant school kids, whole neighborhoods left out. Our nationally lauded Minnesota school systems that leave American Indian kids at the bottom. Nationally. Our disrespected president, our dividing lines, these divided states.

Where in all of this is Indigenous history and presence made visible? Why is it not?

Indigenous stories center our cultures, especially in Minnesota. And yet, to the rest of the world, our stories are not told at all or are told as one myth of one vanishing race. "But you are all dead!"—most Indigenous people hear at some point in our lives. Our stories have been written over with more convenient tales since first contact with Europeans. This narrative includes myths about war (this country was won fair and square) and peace (treaties were signed and "The Indians" sold their land), stories that shorthand white domination without having to admit it. As a nation, we tell these simple stories, in fact we tell the same story for the hundreds of tribes, the three-hundred-plus legal treaties, and so make a lie of the complex and ongoing relationship between our nations and our other nation, the U.S. government. What all of this amounts to is a determined denial of a violent and colonial history that includes not only slavery and segregation but, before that, the genocide and dispossession of Indigenous people that eventually required the import of slaves.

You see now how we have to be invisible? How we must be made ghosts, shadows of the nineteenth century or occasionally haunts risen up out of burial grounds beneath suburban homes—angry, but never avenged, just put back to rest? We have to be vanished, or our national consciousness would have to admit the Indigenous subjugation that makes possible all erasure and absenting, all exclusiveness and owning. If the nation were to ask where Indigenous people are now, a whole different story would start to be told, and it would have to include the clash of cultural realities around the notion of owning, which is decidedly an import. In Europe, rulers owned almost everything. When Europeans came here, they found Indigenous people who lived in relationship to place, who belonged to the land rather than the land belonging to them. This was the land of opportunity for newcomers. Here, anyone, not just the royalty, could take ownership. If you can own land, you can own people. The concept simply extends. If you can make a country out of ownership, you can carry weapons to protect what you own and you can *stand your own ground*.

For many people what I've said above starts to ring some bells. Maybe not for you. Maybe you are one of many who have just become alive to racially motivated police violence and you protest. You may begin to understand that you have lived in or near but have just imagined a world where the rest of us struggle. But perhaps you thought we struggle to be like you, to attain your world, only in our brown or brownish way, our slightly different, but-we-are-all-still-human way. Why wouldn't you think that? I have thought that. No, I have not. I have thought three-quarters of that thought. Work in the system, I was taught. To change the system, work within it, until it includes everyone. Turns out, that work doesn't work well. Turns out, our attempts to work in the system are often just work. Labor. Building of economy on brown and Black bodies. The same labor exploits that sparked the American dream of owning the white picket fence and all it keeps in. What is that fence meant to keep out? I think I know.

Blank again. A mirror, unreflecting, but a sense of the unknown begins to resolve into clarity.

———————

What I know: Native Americans are most likely to suffer police brutality, to die in custody, to be raped by police, to die before police arrive.[1] Give me a statistic and we are at the bottom or the dire top. That cannot matter currently. But it does. Still, I know I'm not the best person to point out that Indigenous people share a disparity with Black lives. My son walks the streets free, and you won't catch

———————

[1] Center for Disease Control and Prevention, Fatal Injury Data, 1999–2013, as reported by Zak Cheney-Rice in "The Police are Killing One Group at a Staggering Rate and Nobody is Talking about It," *Identities.Mic*, February 5, 2015.

me slapping sense into him for protesting. I'll take him to that protest without fear—and I have. *He* was not maced.[2]

Indigenous being has been absent in the conversation on race in this year of Black Lives Matter. And I understand why. My empathy is aimed toward African Americans in this regard, but should it be? When a social media campaign #NativeLivesMatter launched, it was met with marked and at times unpleasant, even uninformed resistance from people associated with Black Lives Matter. That I also understand. A people on fire has no time to fan other people's flames.

One day a Black female poet posted on social media that anyone who is not Black should "sit down and listen" and the same for any woman who has not feared for the Black body of her child. It was all Black and white. And, given the choices offered, I was, suddenly, white.

I've been lying about my race my whole life. I've never lied about my race.

I have come to the point (again) where I must confront my own whiteness, and to do so I must lie to myself that I am white. It's a neat trick, a kind of contortionist shift, like tucking my head beneath my elbow and peeking out. But how else can I get to that other point of view, and how else will I know?

I learned this trick long ago. When I was a girl, a young teen, I got a scholarship to a tony private school and I left home. My hometown on the North Dakota–Minnesota border was white and Red. There was one Black couple. I do not think I had ever spoken to anyone with an African American sensibility before I landed in

---

[2] In May 2015, an African American mother in Baltimore was videotaped striking her young adult son about the head and face as he participated in a protest of police violence to African Americans. A few weeks later in Minneapolis, police sprayed a ten-year-old African American boy with mace during a peaceful protest.

a dorm they called *The Ghetto*. The group that took me in called me *Incog Negro*. It was funny and apt: somehow they knew my looks did not explain all of me. I did go about *incognito* as white, but I was not. I heard what would not be said to a Black person's face, and, if need be, I'd let my friends know. I was the inside outsider. I have been so many times since. I have been so ever since.

My mind goes to race, and it always has because it comforts me. Even in a coffee shop in Minnesota I see race: several Asian American people and one immigrant Chinese man, one young Black woman—possibly she'd say she's mixed. The majority in the café are young white women. There are several men I'd say have origins in the Middle East—because I heard them speak. Equal numbers of apparently white men line the side of the shop where you can plug in your laptop.

And me? I am invisible. I'm part of the invisible tribe.

Erase a people and eventually the erasers will forget them and think the world they stole from the invisible group was theirs for the taking. Once you can own land, you can own people. Once you make Indigenous people fade out of the story, what's left is a whiter white. A wash so opaque Black looks white. Red goes blank. Impossible.

This is impossible to write. It is impossible for me to write on race at this time in American (U.S.) life. I could never say our trouble trumps your trouble. Whoever you are. It is not even to say this is your trouble—it is *our* trouble. Trouble enough for all, these days. In the old days, postwar, we were so proud we had liberated Jewish people from genocide. And what of the country where the atrocities were done? At first, silence—then they told. They told. Many nations tell the stories of their pasts and grow past shame. Telling Indigenous truth, which is a national truth, is not to deny the crisis at hand. It is not to deny my unearned ease in a time of real dis-ease. I know what is not mine. There are ways in which a kind of fear is a particularly Black fear—unknowable to me. I cannot totally understand the fear, the terror, of the Black mother for her son in the era of incarceration. My mind and heart can bend to empathy, no further.

These utterances are impossible and preposterous, and I regret them the instant I write them. I want to go back to my blank space. Yet it seems important to say something for people like me. Something about the story we are forgetting and the way in which our story, Indigenous stories, are the ground upon which all race crimes are committed. Because we do not know where we stand when we stand our ground.

I want to show my mind and fill a blank at once. I am trying to hold it all in one mind, which is already more than two, which is already many. I am trying to tell you how it is now, well into a century of hate crime and police profiling. How it is now harder than ever—while I check my skin privilege, while I ally and advocate, but hang back and be silent and sit and listen—to find room for my racial border-dwelling, which is based in this place before borders, the real haunted ground that only truth will avenge and telling reconcile. The untold land where our national problem with race arose and where it still lives.

You would think
(divide described)
I live like this
One thing on one side

Wrong
Nothing like one side
Or another side
not there or there

Here
I live
Here

Here
We live
Here

Where you live

THE GOOD KIND OF IMMIGRANTS

JaeRan Kim

JaeRan Kim is assistant professor at University of Washington Tacoma. JaeRan's writing and scholarship focuses on the intersections of race, disability, gender, and kinship of vulnerable children and families.

I sometimes believe it was my destiny to be born many times like a cat, whose lives steal away on silent, soft paws. Reincarnation holds a special appeal, the leaving of the old and used in order to birth a fresh and new self. A cat's lives end at nine; as a transnational adoptee, however, I could be born again as often as I wished or others imposed upon me. Snakes shed their old selves in long, translucent sleeves, so delicate that they disintegrate quickly, so quickly that soon there is no memory left at all. I was not left to die but left to be born again and again. First, born nameless to a woman with no name or face. Then wrapped in a quilted jacket in a box on the steps of a provincial city hall in South Korea. Re-born as a child of God into the arms of Saint Mary and White Lily Orphanage. I became #7139 by the second orphanage's adoption agency. Gestated through the sky on the lap of the adoption escort who crowned me over the threshold of an airplane's door and into the waiting arms of my adoptive parents.

I have very few memories of the day I arrived in Minnesota as a toddler. There are the barest of fragments, more sensory than anything; I remember a lot of crying, other children crying. I think they were babies. I recall sitting in someone's lap, a woman's lap. I was stoic, trying to survive, not sure if the wails were mine.

Mostly, I don't remember. I don't remember the people who

raised me for the first year of my life. I don't remember life in two orphanages, one rural and one urban. I don't remember leaving the orphanage or how many of us boarded the airplane destined for Minnesota that July day in 1971. I don't remember meeting my new adoptive parents or how it felt to be swept into the arms of these two unfamiliar people and the others, my soon-to-be relatives, crowding around them crying and laughing and talking to me in a language I did not understand. The yellow-hued photographs from that day show only a tiny, stiff, wide-eyed child in a vanilla-colored Sears, Roebuck dress with a "HOLT" orphanage patch hand-stitched on the front placket.

I don't remember how it felt to lose my *bomo*, my orphanage caregiver, and the other children in my room at the orphanage. I don't remember how I felt that first night enjoying the privileges of adoption, a room of my own, in the suburban Minneapolis home of my "forever family." I don't remember learning to eat American food, but I quickly learned to forget the tastes of my homeland. My adoptive mother recalls that I had an insatiable appetite. She had never known a child so young who could eat four fried eggs in a row; it was as if, she said, I was making up for lost time. Twenty years after my adoption, I sat in a Korean restaurant and ate *kimchi*, only I had forgotten the taste and spit it out, the hot chili pepper and sourness of the cabbage that once felt like home now unfamiliar, burning my mouth. It would take a few years of trying again and again before my palate stopped rejecting the flavors. I still have an insatiable appetite. I am still hungry, and I still cannot remember.

I am one of the estimated 15,000 Korean-born children sent to Minnesota through adoption. Minnesota is not particularly known for its robust Korean American community, however. In 1970, the year before I was adopted, an estimated 38,000 lived in the United States in total. Because the census did not count Koreans as a separate ethnic group in Minnesota, it is unknown how many lived here, but it is likely the numbers were low. In 2010 Minnesota's Korean population was just under 21,000 according to the U.S. Census, making Korean adoptees the majority of the Korean population in Minnesota. Minnesota did have one notable Korean American, however; Mrs. Hyun Sook Han, a social worker trained at the University of Minnesota's school of social work.[1] Mrs. Han served as liaison between South Korea and Minnesota, establishing a relationship between the two places, developing Minnesota's reputation for being home to the largest number of Korean adoptions in the United States.

The setting for my own transracial and transnational adoption experience, however, had already been contextually laid in place by a number of factors prior to Mrs. Han's work at the local Children's Home Society of Minnesota. For the first half of the twentieth century it was generally considered best practice to place a child into a home where the adopted child was similar in physical features, ethnic heritage, religious background, and assumed intelligence to the prospective adoptive parents in a process and philosophy that smacks of eugenics.[2] Yet the United States also has a long history of using child adoption as a means of assimilating populations considered "uncivilized," including undesired immigrants as well as Indigenous tribal nations. Placing immigrant and Indigenous children into certain kinds of white families and institutions sped up the assimilation process desired by the U.S. government and an Anglo-Protestant citizenry. The Native American boarding schools and the orphan train movement were projects of assimilation, using children as the means of excising an undesired culture.

Adoption serves as a project of nation building at two levels: the intimate sphere of private family building and the public, national-level aims of growing a robust citizenry. Raising a child is symbolic. Raising a child burdened with the mark of "otherness" as a full American patriot is heroic. The conflict of "matching" children to adoptive parents was mediated in part by the

---

[1] Hyun Sook Han and Kari Ruth, *Many Lives Intertwined: A Memoir* (St. Paul, MN: Yeong & Yeong, 2004).

[2] Ellen Herman, *Kinship by Design: A History of Adoption in the Modern United States* (Chicago: University of Chicago Press, 2008).

discourse and construction of adopting "other" children as charity and rescue. How else could we understand why white adults like my adoptive parents, with no personal or social connection to communities of color and with no plan to establish these connections in the future, bring a child of color into their homes and neighborhoods except to believe they were doing it as an action of saving a child?

A couple of years ago my adoptive mother spread out a pile of faded, yellowed documents on her dining room table. Shuffling black and white photographs and letters filled with the sharply curled calligraphy of generations ago, her eyes skimming the scattered bits of papers and images, she searched for the information she hoped would confirm to me the news she had recently learned. My mother has been investigating her family's genealogy for some time now. Neutral about my search for information about my Korean heritage and family, she is nonetheless proud about "our" family's connection to Oliver Wolcott, one of the original signatories of the Declaration of Independence. I understand the desire to know one's historical roots and to see oneself reflected within a larger family tree. I also understand how it feels to discover that a part of that family tree is either untrue or missing; to have to reconsider the veracity of those historical bricks upon which you have built your identity.

In my mother's case, her paternal side of the family tree was well documented, back to that Oliver Wolcott and all. But on her maternal side, apparently some of the family tree was grafted. My mother had recently learned through an offhand remark by her aunt that her beloved Granny O'Neal, her great-grandmother, may have been adopted from an orphan train. As an adoption scholar, I often talk about the historical contexts of my work; this created a potential new connection between a great-great-grandmother I knew only from stories and me, via adoption.

In the midst of the industrial revolution in the United States, urban cities in the East Coast struggled with the influx of immigrants seeking opportunity in America. In many of these places, the increase in immigrants impacted cities' ability to keep up with necessary infrastructure and support. Families lived in over-crowded tenement buildings, creating the perfect environment for spreading disease and illness en masse. Industries could not keep up with demand for employment. Children were orphaned or left to fend for themselves while parents attempted to find work. Many children were sent out into the streets to find work to help support their families. The growing numbers of immigrant families—not merely those who landed at Ellis Island but also the rising number of children born to immigrant families—presented a growing concern to the urban middle class and elite. Left on their own, these impoverished, uneducated, and unsupervised children would, as Presbyterian minister and founder of the New York Children's Aid Society Charles Loring Brace predicted, become the "dangerous classes of New York."

Brace's imagined ideal setting to teach a child about a life of wholesome hard work and prosperity: the farm. And so, from 1853 until 1929, an estimated 250,000 children were gathered from these dangerous, urban city streets and sent by train to rural farming communities where they were put up on platforms and chosen by local families in what seemed at the time to be a win-win scenario. Poor children would learn the values of the humble Protestant farmer by working on the farms or, for the girls, in domestic work in exchange for room and board. Minnesota was the site of several stops in the orphan train itinerary; an estimated four thousand children were plucked off the train platforms and went to live with Minnesota farming families.

Protestant ethics and bucolic farm life aside, there were larger goals involved. On the surface, the orphan train movement was partly about improving the lives of children in need, but more so represented the concern at the time that these children would grow up to become a burden on society. Anti-immigrant sentiment was high, particularly against Catholic and Jewish immigrants. It is no surprise then that the vast majority of the children involved were Catholic and Jewish immigrants. And, although the rhetoric guiding the orphan train movement made it sound like these children were being adopted or fostered, the reality was that these children experienced a life more along the lines of indentured labor, working in exchange for room and board until they reached the age of majority. Not all of the children were adopted or fostered, but most permanently lost their roots and original family information.

If it's true that my great-great-granny O'Neal was Irish Catholic by birth, she became Irish Protestant once placed with the midwestern O'Neal family. There are no birth certificates or adoption records that would hint at her origins; most of the children were placed on the train without any documentation. It is unknown whether her family of origin, if alive, had agreed to let her be placed on the train. Brace and his compatriots did not always verify that the children had living family members. Children were routinely taken from orphanages, where it was assumed that they had been abandoned, and those taken off the streets were assumed to have unfit parents not worth consulting about their child's future. Like the Native American boarding schools housing Indigenous children forcibly removed from their family and tribal communities, changing an orphan train child's name, religion, and ethnic heritage through an upbringing in the dominant culture is one way to ensure the erasure of the child's cultural and spiritual differences. Indeed, my great-great-grandmother and I had much in common.

Transracial and Transnational Adoption

Minnesota seems an unlikely state for transracial and transnational adoption. Minnesota is known for its lakes and farms, livable urban cities, and beautiful North Shore. Minnesota is not known for its racial diversity, particularly outside the Twin Cities. To be a Korean adoptee in Minnesota is to be both hypervisible and invisible at the same time. It means that people can tell you they don't see you as Korean as if that is a compliment. Translation: you are not one of *those* Asians, the ones who have a heavy accent or don't speak English, who eat smelly food, practice a strange religion, have too many children, or refuse to act "American." Being a transracial adoptee means being a race-traitor every day and having to accept that this makes you more likable. Being a transracial adoptee in Minnesota is having people expect you to say thank you when they tell you how "articulate" you are. Being a Korean adoptee in Minnesota means having to explain your personal adoption stories to people you don't know because no one understands how you can be from Plymouth or St. Cloud or Moorhead or Rochester when asked, "Where are you from? No, where are you *really* from?" My own journey to Minnesota is situated as part of a larger Minnesota ethic of democratic labor–inspired colorblindness. In addition, my adoption could only occur because it was built on a historical context that positioned Korean adoptees as acceptable diversity because of, as historian Arissa Oh suggests, our "non-blackness."[3]

The first transnational adoptions to the United States were the adoptions of German, Greek, and Japanese children sent to the United States following World War II and up through the early 1950s. Although the number of these adoptions was small, and many of the Japanese children were mixed race as a result of having American GI fathers, it is surprising that any white, U.S. couple was willing to adopt a Japanese child given that the adoption practices of the time favored racial and ethnic matching and the political and racial context was one of high anti-Japanese sentiment. The internment of Japanese Americans did not fully end until 1946. Additionally, because federal immigration laws imposed strict quotas and exclusions for Asian immigration until 1965, Japanese children immigrating via adoption were an exception, as were Korean children.

The transracial adoptions of Japanese children were not the only adoptions of children across race. Minnesota is the unlikely setting for the first officially recorded transracial adoption of a black child to white parents in the United States. The adoption occurred in 1948 and the placement was made by Laura Gaskins,

---

[3] Arissa Oh, *To Save the Children of Korea: The Cold War Origins of International Adoption* (Redwood City, CA: Stanford University Press, 2015).

the first African American social worker to be hired at Hennepin County. According to Gaskins, "Black parents were hard to recruit because of the small number living in the area. When no black home could be located for him, and when a white family wanted very much to adopt him, I decided to place him in this permanent home."[4] In a time of "matching" in adoption and Jim Crow America, this placement was an unconventional one to say the least. In addition, from 1958 to 1967, nearly four hundred Native American children, including children from Minnesota, were placed in white adoptive homes as part of the Indian Adoption Project.

Michelle was dark haired and brown eyed, small like me, although she was sturdier and stockier than me. We met in kindergarten, and she lived nearby, across Old Highway 12 in a white, two-story traditional house with green trim. I'd heard a rumor that her uncle was a famous wrestler on television, and although I wasn't aware of the wrestling world or her uncle, her proximity to fame was enough to impress me. We were friends for a couple of years and then, as people do, moved into different circles. I lived a short distance from my junior high school, and one morning on my way to school I heard someone call my name. Michelle was also a walker and, having a few more blocks to walk than I, had seen me up ahead. I waited for her and from that day on we began walking together, separating into our different cliques once we arrived at school. By the time we moved on to high school I had lost touch with her once again.

Many years later I would meet a woman who knew Michelle. I would learn that Michelle struggled with addiction and homelessness after high school. I had no idea that Michelle was a transracial adoptee, or that she was Native American, and I still don't know of her tribal lineage. I learned she often traversed the sidewalks near the corner of Franklin and Cedar near the Little Earth community down the street from my neighborhood begging for spare change from the commuters, and I was struck by the

---

[4] Joyce Ladner, *Mixed Families: Adopting across Racial Boundaries* (Garden City, NY: Anchor Press/Doubleday, 1977).

knowledge that I had probably driven past her many times. Even now when I drive by, I look for her face in every Native American woman I see, hoping to recognize her. When we were children, adoption had never come up for discussion between us, and I wonder if she even knew I was adopted, just as I had no clue about her adoption. Consciously or not, even as children we did what any Minnesotan would have done—considered it too impolite to ask outright. Just as in junior high, we were able to walk only so far together before our paths diverged.

Becoming Minnesotan

Raised on a diet of *Little House on the Prairie* and *A Prairie Home Companion*, two narratives with unequivocal Minnesota settler colonial themes, I grew up feeling as if I inhabited life in Walnut Grove or Lake Wobegon—rural Midwest townships with generic Lutheran values fully absent of Indigenous communities, much less anyone without a surname suffix of *-son*. I wanted to be where "all the women are strong, all the men are good looking, and all the children are above average." We didn't attend a Lutheran church, but Lake Wobegon descriptions of church basement fruit gelatin salads dotted with mini-marshmallows, canned soup–based hot dishes, and dessert bars are the memories of my childhood. Despite what felt like an overabundance of the show's bluegrass and gospel-lite, not something I associated with Minnesota's music scene, Garrison Keillor's stories of life in Lake Wobegon and descriptions of the Lutheran ethic always felt true. *Prairie Home Companion* was the familiar cultural touchstone on family vacations, always reminding us of home. Even if we could not find a church to attend on our summer travels, we could count on the *Prairie Home Companion* rebroadcast on Sunday.

In second grade I discovered *Little House in the Big Woods* and hungrily read through the entire Little House series, then reread the books so often that the covers were torn and the pages dog-eared and smudged. Laura Ingalls was my soul sister, and I was thrilled when my maternal grandmother made me a hand-sewn bonnet and dress just like what Laura would have worn. I identified with Laura in so many ways: her sometimes tense relationship with her perfect sister Mary with the golden curls, a loving but stern and no-nonsense mother, and a playful and adventurous father. Like Laura, I felt my blonde-haired sister was too perfect. She didn't express angry feelings, whereas I seemed unable to control my emotions. Like Laura, I wanted to be good but seemed unable to control my impulses. Every feeling was clearly expressed through my face. I also undervalued my mother, who was burdened with caring for three young children while my gregarious and fun-loving father spent days working and evenings volunteering for a number of local civic and social groups.

My favorite book in the series was *On the Banks of Plum Creek*, set in the time period when the Ingalls family lived in Walnut Grove, Minnesota. In this book, Laura experiences being an outsider for the first time. When Nellie Oleson mocks her for being a "country girl," I felt I knew exactly what Laura felt. I was always the outsider, the Asian girl with the white parents, the girl the other kids on the playground circled chanting, "Chinese, Japanese, dirty knees, look at these!" I wanted to believe that Laura's history was my own history, that I also had deep roots in this country instead of the fragile, transplanted roots from my recent immigration. Back then I had no conception of settler colonialism, the process by which families like the Ingalls occupied and laid personal claim to land after driving out the Indigenous peoples, nor did I recognize the racism embedded in a child's version of pioneer life. It's embarrassing that while I continued to read the Little House books periodically throughout my entire childhood and adolescence, it wasn't until college that I realized how much racism was in the series—and how similarly I overlooked the racism of my childhood embedded in the culture of Minnesota wholesomeness.

The "good" immigrants of my childhood were Scandinavian and two generations removed. In my paternal grandmother's dining room, a browned shellacked wooden plaque of the Norwegian table prayer hung on the wall.

I Jesu navn gar vi til bords
a spise, drikke pa ditt ord.
Deg, Gud til aere, oss til gavn,
Sa far vi mat i Jesu navn.
Amen.

I would often stand in front of the plaque and try to guess how the words would sound. The oldest daughter of Norwegian immigrants, Grandma Nelson was raised on a farm in northern Minnesota. She did not know a word of English until she went to school. By the time I arrived, her Norwegian was dusty and mostly forgotten, though if you listened carefully the faint remnants of Norwegian occasionally curled around the edges of her northern Minnesota accent. I once asked her if she would say the Norwegian prayer instead of our usual grace before dinner. To my surprise, she agreed, tripping a little bit over the words. It was one of the few times I felt connected to her.

Unlike my maternal grandparents, Grandma Nelson wasn't on board with my parents adopting a Korean child—but then again, she was opposed to my uncle's marriage to a Catholic woman. I think she loved me in her own way, but she wasn't affectionate like my other grandma, who was round and soft and looked like a hug. Grandma Nelson was thin, stoic, and judgmental. I was afraid of her. Maybe I was aware we were more alike than I would have wished.

We were both the *good* kind of immigrants: she the daughter of Norwegian Lutherans invested in the American dream, and I the adopted Asian child, rescued and saved from Communism and "from the cold and misery and darkness of Korea," as my adoption papers state. We accepted the price of being American—to assimilate completely, our first tongue relegated to a decorative plaque on the wall. Except unlike Great-great-granny O'Neal and Grandma Nelson, my physical appearance would never allow me to become fully assimilated. There were always people willing to remind me that I was not a "real American."

Red and yellow, black and white, all are precious in his sight

On a yellow school bus chartering children home from summer bible camp, I became a born-again Christian somewhere on the black ribbon of Highway 10 between Brainerd and Plymouth. The day was hot and humid, as August in Minnesota always is, and, dotted with mosquito bites and feverish with the Lord, I closed my eyes and silently prayed that God would forgive my sins and allow me to be born again. And then, unsure of whether God had truly heard my prayer, I repeated. I repeated the prayer the same way I would shampoo my hair twice in case I didn't get all the dirt out on the first try.

At eight years old, I had borne witness to becoming born again many times. Each Sunday, Pastor Childs would give the "invitation" to become a child of God. As a child of the earth made of blood and skin and the bone of Adam's rib, I was a lost soul abandoned and in need of the Heavenly Father's grace. This I understood well; not only had I been physically abandoned on the steps of Daegu City Hall in South Korea, I'd been spiritually abandoned as well. If anyone understood the gift I had been given by my adoption, it was I. If Moses could lead his people despite being sent downstream, why would I deny the spiritual gifts in store for me?

Still, I had hesitated. Eyes must be squeezed tightly shut, or the temptation to peek would be too difficult to resist. Growing up in the church, I noticed people clasped their hands in prayer in different ways. Some interlaced the fingers, wrapping them around the backs of each opposing hand, tightly wound in a ball. Others pressed palms and fingers together, mirror image, rigid with righteousness. Occasionally when one of the black churches' gospel choirs from Minneapolis came to perform for our congregation, a few people would raise their arms, elbows bent and hands tipped back the way we held the bar in the bent-arm test for the President's Physical Fitness Test, shake their heads side to side, and utter "Amen!" But mostly, people at my church were solemn, respectful. Private. They held their clasped hands low, arms hugging the front of their waists.

Jesus loves the little children,
All the children of the world.
Red and yellow, black and white,
All are precious in His sight,
Jesus loves the little children of the world.

At summer camp, I became fast friends with Kim, another girl who was also adopted from Korea. We stayed up late, lying on our stomachs in Kim's top bunk, sharing secrets. After several days of being asked if we were twins, we started to promote the idea around camp. Once, when a bratty boy asked me if we knew *kung-fu* I said yes and kicked him in the shin. We felt as badass as two eight-year-olds at a Christian summer camp in rural Minnesota possibly could.

Christian summer camp, and church in general, was where I learned about sin and redemption; it is also where I experienced the most overt visibility as a transracial adoptee. Though I kept my eyes lowered, every time I sang, "Red and yellow, black and white, all are precious in his sight," I felt the heat of stares as the only "yellow" in the room. Boys in their dirty swim trunks and tousled sand-covered hair followed me around camp chanting, "Kawasaki, Mitsubishi!" My white friends giggled, thinking they were following me because they had a crush on me. When their eyebrows raised as I responded, "Ford, Chrysler, ha, ha!" I had to explain the boys were racist, not horny. Although now I understand they were likely both.

The church was never a sanctuary of grace and understanding for me, but rather a space where my awareness of difference was heightened. I was not immune to name-calling, eye-pulling, and chants of "ching-chong" by the other kids at Sunday school. Diversity meant white missionaries presenting slideshows of their work with people of color in so-called "heathen" countries, youth group excursions to the "inner city," code for a predominantly black neighborhood, or the occasional gospel choir providing a little energy to our staid congregation. The few of us who were not white were mostly transracially adopted children. I was the symbol that evangelism in "third-world" countries worked. I was an unwanted child from a heathen country. Church was a reminder that as a Korean and an adoptee, I was expected to be doubly grateful for being saved.

Epilogue

White Lily Orphanage no longer exists. The buildings and grounds are the same today as they were when I was a resident, but the orphanage now houses a daycare center. When I visit, the children's shoes are lined up in rows outside their classroom, and I imagine my own shoes once nestled among them. Sister Grace is in full habit and wimple; she pulls out photo albums dating back to my time at White Lily but can't find me in any of the photographs. Once again, I am invisible, there but not really there.

My husband and children have joined me on this trip. After touring the old orphanage I take them to see the statue of Mary, still standing in the lawn surrounded by flowers at her feet. My children, raised on Disney films about orphans with dead mothers, cannot reconcile the mother they know with the child who once lived here. We go to city hall where I was abandoned and sit on the steps where I am told I was found by a night watchman. A Korean man sees us, wonders why we are sitting on the steps. How do I explain to a stranger why we are there, that I need to offer my children some sense of their roots, even if I never succeed in finding the actual place or people who birthed me? The kind man offers to take our photograph.

Back home in Minneapolis, we make an album from the trip to Korea. And there it is, the picture of my family on the steps of Daegu City Hall. This, as it turns out, is my salvation. My adoptive parents did what their social workers advised; I cannot blame them for assimilating me and erasing my Korean heritage. Yet I lost more than a set of birth parents when I was adopted to Minnesota—I lost a culture, a heritage, a language, a community, a sense of identity. My children have grown up in a very diverse community in Minnesota. I could not bear to have them experience the same sense of racial isolation I lived growing up in the suburbs. When I read *Little House on the Prairie* to them, we talk about the racism—of Ma's hatred of Native Americans and Pa's blackface minstrel show. When we visit a hotel in Duluth, my daughter remarks on the racist Tiki-themed waterpark. *Prairie Home Companion* holds little appeal. Lake Wobegon is a world they do not know. They know where I, thus we, came from. I do not need to be born again, for my history and future live on in my children, who remember.

FIGHTING THE OPPRESSIVE WHITENESS

Rodrigo Sanchez-Chavarria

Rodrigo Sanchez-Chavarria is a writer and spoken word poet of Peruvian heritage involved with Palabristas, a Minnesota-based Latin@ poets collective. He is an MFA student at Hamline University and writes about fatherhood, the duality of two cultures in English, Spanglish, and Spanish, and issues pertaining to his community.

When someone asks me what it's like to live in Minnesota, I respond, "Fighting the oppressive whiteness all day long." This is a reference to a Key and Peele comic skit that takes place in Minnesota in the midst of a winter storm in which "Black Ice" is criminalized and profiled by the white anchors, as black people are criminalized and oppressed in today's society. The weatherman and the reporter (Key and Peele) defend "Black Ice" and make very intriguing points about being surrounded by whiteness. This, to me, is a metaphor for what it's like at times to live in Minnesota. In reality, if you live in Minnesota and you are a person of color, you have to deal with "oppressive whiteness" quite often—in social parameters, social media, work settings, academia, and the weather.

The irony of the Key and Peele skit is that it is real. I've experienced it, from being followed by security at shopping malls when I was a teenager to being harassed and profiled by Roseville police because I looked too brown for that side of town and required investigating. Being addressed by coworkers with a name different from my own, because to them brown people all look alike; therefore we must have the same names. That does not include the countless times I was referred to as a "spic," "beaner," "rice picker," "dirty Mexican," and many other derogatory terms throughout my upbringing. Before the reader starts thinking that this is a let's-bash-Minnesota essay, let me begin to say that Minnesota has been good to me. I have created community within in its cracked sidewalks, I am raising a family, and I found a partner who challenges me and completes me. But Minnesota introduced me to the idea of "racism."

Back in 1988—this is part of my origin story—my parents knew that in order to give us a better future than the turbulent situation in Peru, we needed to leave. Alan Garcia was about to send the country into an economic crisis that would take ten years to recover from. The Shining Path was at its peak of activity, and I was in fourth grade and had just learned how to take the two buses to get to school all by myself. So my parents took the biggest gamble in their lives and started to sell all of their possessions. My dad sold his Yamaha receiver and his Sony floor speakers that filled our Saturdays of joy, music, and family—and my mother sold the house my grandma had given her. They sold all things they held dear, because our future was their biggest investment. I painfully remember when they were ridiculed by the committee at the embassy with words like, "Why would you want to go there and be poor?" "You will not be able to feed your family on a student's wage." As I heard these words, my first reaction was to go punch these people in the face, but my father's stern stare telegraphed to me that this wasn't the time or the place for that. The restraint both my parents showed during this whole event really was impressive. My mother was outspoken, and my father, when he needed to, would let his actions do the talking. That sometimes meant fists would fly. But regardless, to take a verbal beating like that really taught me about perseverance.

My family was not considered poor, but that does not mean we didn't know what that was. Our neighborhood had electricity and water shortages all the time, candles and buckets filled our apartment for whenever they were needed. I knew what violence looked like; I had seen it with my own eyes. But I was not aware of what racism was until we arrived in Minnesota.

It was in the halls of Brimhall Elementary where I learned what being different meant. It was not only our economic status that gave me a clear disadvantage, but also my lack of fluent English. Mix those two together with serious trips to Savers or Goodwill for clothing, and I was instantly at a social disadvantage in the classroom. It also did not help that this was the largest number of white people I had ever been exposed to. In Peru, the majority of people looked like me, bronze skin kissed by Inti's rays. Peru's Afro-Peruvian history is strong, proud, and vibrant, and I was aware of that, but blue eyes, blond hair were only images I had seen on TV screens. Immediately, I became the outcast in the classroom. People would ask me questions, and all I could answer was *yes* or *no*, so that developed into a game at the lunch table, in which people would ask me questions and I would have to respond. I was their entertainment, their appetizer, if you will. It reminds me a lot of the scene in the show *Fresh Off the Boat* when Eddie Huang sits at the lunch table for the first time and is made fun of because of the smell of the food his mother made him. I spent lonely times at lunch, growing frustrated by not being able to understand what I thought were innocent conversations but later learned were racist comments.

This does not mean that I did not find community. I was fortunate that my parents' endeavors in the academic world of the University of Minnesota meant we had housing at what we could call home for the next seven years, the Commonwealth Terrace Cooperative or, as we all referred to it, the C.T.C. I grew up in an environment that included people from Mexico, Costa Rica, Chile, Brazil, Argentina, and more. It was a perfect commercial for Colors of Benetton. In this dynamic of created community, what we all had in common is that we missed home, and the promise that at one point we would all go back home made adjusting easier. But that wasn't the real world; the reality was that brown people at that time were not as visible as we are today. There was no Lake Street, no Mercado Central, no East Side of St. Paul, no Global Market. The only thing that I considered brown was the West Side of St. Paul, but for a family with no car and unfamiliar with the way mass transit worked, those visits would be few.

There is a notion that needs to be understood here. It takes a certain breed of Person of Color to survive in Minnesota and in the Midwest. While the East Coast and West Coast have established communities that have centuries of history, Minnesota in this case does not. So for someone who comes from one of these established P.O.C. communities, to be able to survive becomes difficult because you cannot find the exact type of community presence. So what does one do to survive? You create the community you are searching for, and you cherish and nurture the fuck out of it. This notion has made me more appreciative of the many communities I consider myself part of, but it also has made me extra protective over them.

If I had understood this better in middle school, I would have saved myself some truly tough times. I really tried to fit in, and by that I mean I tried to not be noticeable. I wanted to be invisible. But that was hard, especially when you could probably gather all the P.O.C. students in one of the smallest classrooms at Roseville Area Middle School. It was in the cafeteria during lunch where I learned about racist epithets. I remember hearing them the first time and feeling numb. Here I am at a lunch table with people I consider friends, and they're calling people names. At first I ignored it, hoping the problem would go away, because I wanted that badly to be accepted. But it only got worse. So I did what felt right. I got up and walked away. I spent lunch either by myself or, if I got lucky, with the outcasts. These events are still vibrant in my memory. How all of these racist comments came from the mouths of white kids. I am not generalizing that all white people are racist, only sharing my experience.

In high school I went through a huge identity crisis. I refused to speak Spanish; I denounced everything I knew about my homeland. I wanted to be a suburban kid, and I would go to great lengths to try to achieve it. Buying discontinued clothes, borrowing clothes from friends who ended up donating the clothes to me, looking for nice tennis shoes in the lost and found or at bargain clothing stores—I tried it all. But all it got me was disappointment after disappointment, with one clear message. Even if I tried, acceptance was not going to happen. I could play the role, but that role was not mine.

It was that summer after ninth grade, the summer I learned to ride a bike, when one of the kids in the neighborhood started becoming louder about his racist ideologies. I remember sitting at a picnic table with a friend of mine when this kid tried to be part of the conversation. I tolerated him as much as I could. We both did, but when he said to me that I was worthless, that he would sell me as his slave at the garage sale they were having the next day, I snapped. I started punching and kicking him from the picnic table all the way to the door of his house. I couldn't stop myself. I kept hearing him say that over and over in my head, and all I could do was keep swinging and keep kicking. When I saw him gasp for air after my last punch to his gut emptied out his breath, I stopped. I realized what I had done. His mother came out and threatened me, and I responded, "Ask him what he called me and what he was going to do to me at your garage sale." As wrong as it was to engage in violence, it was also liberating to be able to silence him. That was not the only time fists had to be used to battle racist comments, but at least we knew, as the P.O.C. kids of the C.T.C., that if needed, we would not hesitate to use them.

Use them we did. Where one weed grows, others will soon sprout, and that analogy applied to this situation. A couple more kids moved into the neighborhood, and they happened to agree with the racist ideology that was infecting our dear C.T.C. And it wasn't uncommon that we would settle the disputes over a game of tackle football or basketball. In honesty, most of these games never lasted too long before fists and insults flew, but we stood our ground, always stood our ground.

We had each other's backs. I vividly remember one instance during the summer where my friend Abner and I were chilling outside by my place. All of a sudden one of those kids called Abner's brother Sam (short for Semhar) the N word, and before we could jump into action, Sam started beating the life out of the kid from the basketball courts to his house up and down the hills, through playground equipment and sandboxes—as if the fight was a last straw to the "Go home you dirty [insert racist epithet]!" we grew accustomed to hearing from these individuals on a daily basis.

And then there were the police. For every act of vandalism that happened in the C.T.C., we were always Suspect Number One. I was fixing my bike, a bike I spent the summer building. We were all gathered on our bikes in the parking lot, and all of a sudden I heard sneakers screeching and bike chains rattling. I looked up and saw, creeping slowly with no sirens, a police car. I quickly got on my bike and pedaled away as fast as I could. I kept saying to myself, "Why are we running? We didn't do anything wrong." It wasn't until I met up with the rest of the group that I realized none of us knew why we ran away. We just did, because that is all we knew to do. Decades later I would realize that we ran because we had been harassed and profiled by the police so many times that our subconscious at that moment had gone from thinking to "fight or flight" mode. Since we were taught not to fight the police, we ran. I was glad I convinced the group to go back home, since we didn't do anything wrong. When we did, we found our parents arguing with the police. The officer started to threaten us that he was about to put out an APB on us. It was a sight to see. Immigrant parents from different countries defending us. A mini United Nations in our own backyard. I would remember this moment vividly, as it reminded me to fight and question.

Fight and question I did. In 2008, as I headed to El Paso, Texas, for a conference, Minnesota governor Tim Pawlenty was throwing his hat into the immigration debate with a proposition that would have police officers enforce immigration laws—ask people about their immigration status, with no reason. I had his horrific scheme in my mind as we arrived, and I overheard a group of women discussing which bag was theirs as they were putting their carry-on luggage through the x-ray machine. I quickly replied to them in Spanish that their luggage would be in the order that each of them were scanned by security. As I grabbed my bag, a man came up to me and told me to step aside with him so he could ask me some questions. He started asking about my reason for visiting El Paso and if I had documents proving my citizenship. I angrily challenged him, I asked for *his* documentation, for his badge or identification. He quickly flashed a card that he said identified him as an immigration officer. He showed it to me so fast I could barely read it. I had read somewhere that there were people posing as immigration officers, and this smelled like a scam. I started getting loud, and I said, "If you don't let me go I will grab the attention of my classmates and we will see who really goes with who." At that moment the man released his grip on my arm and walked away. I was reminded that day of how my friends' parents fought for us against the accusation of the police that night and how that fight was a fight for existence and survival.

This perhaps was the foreshadowing for myself, always fighting. Ever since we moved here, it feels like we have had to fight for our right to exist. Always in some way countering the "oppressive whiteness," in all the forms it decides to present itself. None were found more in abundance than in college. By then I had created a plan that I would use to defend against blatant racism—you know, the racist epithets and stereotypes being projected at you by people who will claim they are not racist because they have a friend who is black, yellow, red, brown. People who own that mentality are better off using the excuse that they are not racist because they own a color TV. At least that way we both can laugh at the ludicrous statement, and hopefully they can start to realize the error in their ways, but more than likely that is not what will happen. What is more likely is that I will be accused of being overly sensitive and extremely politically correct. Being told to relax and not take things seriously, to not be so reverse-racist. But why shouldn't I be sensitive to it? The bigger question is why do they believe it is not offensive? Because they come from a position of privilege, a position of power. We must understand that racism is based on power. Whoever has it determines what the rules are, and if you haven't noticed, people of color have not been in the position to make those decisions.

This of course is present in the academic realm, whether it be in the form of Goldy the Gopher wearing a serape at a university-sponsored student event, or not funding a Chicano and Latino Studies department with the tools to attract faculty and increase its curriculum, or not supporting your faculty of color when three white students file a discrimination complaint against them. All these things and more I've witnessed, and that is why organizations like Voices for Racial Justice and their Legislative Report Card on Racial Equity are important in Minnesota. It is important to keep fighting, because without struggle there is no change.

My mother told me that I was born in the wrong generation, that I would have been perfect in her generation, when you needed to fight to exist. I told my mom that like her I was born into marches, and my babies were, too. That we have resistance in our blood, we are agitators like her and the people who came before us. We just happen to call Minnesota home.

DARK TREES IN THE LANDSCAPE OF LOVE

Kao Kalia Yang

Kao Kalia Yang is a Hmong American writer and the author of *The Latehomecomer: A Hmong Family Memoir*, published in 2008 by Coffee House Press, and *The Song Poet*, published in 2016 by Metropolitan Books.

I asked my four-year-old nephew Phooj if he liked the leaves on the maple trees, all burning with color, bright oranges, vibrant yellows, and deep reds.

He said, "No. I like black trees, myself."

I said, "Black trees? Where are they?"

He said, "They are everywhere, Auntie Kalia."

His soft child's hand in mine, we went looking. All around us there were trees. The grass, still green from warm summer, was littered with fallen leaves, some dry and crispy, others lush with moisture, holding to dear life. I looked up and around. I couldn't see a black tree anywhere. My eyes shifted from one tree to the next. The colors on the maple trees drew my attention once more. Their leaves were soaked in colors like blazing flames. Beside their vibrancy, the other trees paled—even the bright yellow leaves of the ash trees that petaled the grass and the sidewalk. After fifteen minutes of Phooj holding my hand, letting go, pointing to the cracks in the sidewalk, admiring the flight of an errant bee, occasionally looking up at me, searching my face, and me trying earnestly to see what he saw, I gave up on the search for the black trees.

I said, "I can't see them. Where are they?"

He answered, "They are everywhere, Auntie Kalia."

He smiled up at me. His smile grew bigger, his little white teeth all in a fine row.

Finally, he said, "Look on the street, Auntie Kalia. The black trees are everywhere!"

He pointed to the middle of the street.

All over, I began to see the black trees, their limbs twisting and turning as the wind caused ripples across the leaves. He was referring to the shadows of the trees I had been marveling at, and of the ones I hadn't been paying attention to.

Underneath the bright sunshine, I saw the paleness of Phooj's skin, the light caramel of his eyes, the perfectly aquiline nose, the particular waviness of his hair—departures from my sister's yellow face, dark eyes, straight black hair, and my own.

———

The first time I saw my husband, there was no inkling of a future romance. He had heard me give a public talk. The things I said had resonated. He had sent an e-mail to say as much. I was cordial in my response: "If I can be of use in your work, please let me know." To my surprise, he had written back and asked for a coffee date. I was not partial to coffee, so I suggested lunch. We met at a busy restaurant owned by Hmong folk on University Avenue. It was a casual work meeting so far as I was concerned.

Aaron. He was tall, as most white men are, especially compared to me. He was balding. He wore glasses. He was halfway through a PhD program at the University of Minnesota. He was soft spoken and nervous. He had biked all the way to the restaurant from his home in Minneapolis. He was sweating a lot, rivulets running down his head, down his face. He was really drinking the water. When I approached, he wiped his head nervously with a paper napkin; bits of white, soggy paper clung to his wet skin. We shook hands.

If anyone had suggested that Aaron was the man I would marry, I would have disagreed vehemently. I had always imagined myself with Num Sornram Teppitak, the Thai actor I had loved since I was twelve but who had no clue I was alive, or with a Hmong man. I didn't imagine who the Hmong man would be, as I spent most of my free imagination time on Num; however, I loved the language I had been born into. I grew up understanding romance in the love songs of early Touly Vangkue, Sounders, and Xanakee. The love I wanted was the kind that you could retrieve from a pillow someone has been dreaming on: *Nco txog sijhawm wb tseem nyob ua ib kev, txawm wb txoj kev sib hlub twb dhau mus lawm, thaum kuv ua npau suav pom wb nyob ua kev . . . zoo li wb twb tsis paub hais tias ib hnub wb yuav sib ncaim*; This rose here, it is for you, to signify my love, if it isn't good enough, please still accept still, that it is the love between us, please accept this rose, take it and treasure it, when you miss me. I wanted to be with someone who could understand the words I loved so much, the sentiments I carried every time I saw the transfer of a red rose from one hand to the other, someone who understood that true love was a love that existed as if there would be no parting, ever. Aaron certainly had never heard of these bands or their songs describing the love I wanted to marry, and he was not Num Sornram Teppitak by a long shot.

When we first started hanging out, it was casual and friendly. I needed a good friend, and he was great friend material, with his high intelligence, his appreciation of laughter, his love of language, his easy, no-pressure camaraderie. By the time I realized that perhaps what I felt for him was beyond friendship, I had already ventured far enough into his memories of heartache, pain, and sorrow and the exquisite joy he takes from living in the present that I could no longer dismiss his presence in my life or the idea of a cohesive, shared future. Three months after we met, Aaron proposed.

It was cold and clear and snowy in Andover, Minnesota. I was home alone. I had a dentist appointment in St. Paul. I had a car to get there, but my only pair of glasses was in my father's car. Aaron and I had been on the phone together. He did not like the fact that I wanted to keep my dentist appointment and that I would, with or without the glasses. He insisted on driving me, and despite my objections, he came over. We had a few minutes before the drive. We were sitting on my family's stained micro-fiber sofa, the television was on some daytime talk show, and the room was flooded with sunlight. Without my glasses, I saw circles of light dancing around Aaron's sparkling, bald head.

I said, "You shouldn't have come. I would have been fine."

He said, "I don't want anything to happen to you."

I said, "I can see still cars, you know. I'm not that blind yet."

He said, "I'm here. I'll drive you."

I said, "I don't know why you insist."

He said, "I love you."

He said, "I want to be with you."

I said, "Are you proposing?"

He said, "Yes."

I said, "Do it properly."

He did. The American way. He held my hands, looked into my eyes, and in English said, slowly, "Will you marry me?"

I said, "Sure."

We didn't set a date. He was doing something nice for me. I wanted to do something nice in return. It was between the two of us. It was not a big deal. Engagements are broken daily. Certainly, a semi-proposal was nothing to hold me back should we decide otherwise at any time in the future. That's how I thought of our arrangement.

The snow melted and the green grass grew tall as the crab apple trees budded and unfurled their blooms. Aaron and I continued our relationship. He came to visit often at my family's house. Occasionally I went with him to his parents' house for dinner. Everyone was nice to everyone. The crab apple blooms fell to the ground, grew brown, shriveled, and disappeared. The trees were lush and green, heavy with their summery leaves, when Aaron and I decided to formalize the proposal so that we could take a road trip to Colorado.

I belong to a traditional Hmong family. I wanted to respect the place of my mother and father and the things they had taught me about safety and self-worth. I knew I did not want to go to Colorado with Aaron without their consent and ease of heart.

So, Aaron asked my father and mother for my hand in marriage. My mother was quiet. My father was not. He told Aaron of our poverty, our numbers, and talked of my role and responsibilities as an older child. He told Aaron all my big flaws as a person—my short temper, my tendency to speed, how my large heart often collided with reality and how it raged in response. Aaron assured my father that I was like abalone, worth the effort—except there is no Hmong word for abalone, so my sister ended up translating to my father that Aaron thought I was like shellfish. My father, a Hmong song poet, perhaps intrigued by the comparison of his daughter to shellfish, accepted Aaron's bid for my hand in marriage on behalf of both himself and my mother.

My father said by way of ending the conversation, "Please give yourself time to think of my words. You are welcome to change your mind. No problem."

Aaron's father's words to me were very different. We were eating dinner at his parents' house. There was quiet classical music on in the background. There were low candles twinkling at the center of the table. Aaron's mother had prepared a meal, maybe skirt steak and a salad, warm rolls with butter. I knew that when Aaron's brother-in-law entered the family, things weren't smooth, and he came from similar demographics. I knew that Aaron's father had a conversation with him about his finances and his offerings as a husband. I knew that Aaron's mother had strong reservations about her daughter's choice for a mate. I knew Aaron had told his parents about our decision to formalize the proposal with an engagement. I sat through dinner waiting for the questions to come. There would be no need for translation in this conversation.

Near the end of the meal, Aaron's father said, "Why do you want to marry Aaron?"

I hadn't been eating much to make sure my mouth was empty enough to talk when the time came. I said, "He's kind, caring, and interested in fostering my dreams."

Aaron's mother asked a similar question. I responded in a similar way.

I understood they were looking for reassurances on my feelings about their son. There was no need to talk about finances or professional prospects. I hadn't hidden my financial status in previous conversations. They knew I had no money and that I had student loans. They knew I was a writer, hoping to make a life at it. More importantly, they knew that their son wanted to marry me. These facts did not ease my nervousness but made it easier on my heart.

Aaron and I were married on August 6, 2011. The weather forecasters had predicted a storm that day, but we were lucky. The air was hot and humid, but the rains did not come. About five hundred guests attended our wedding; most were my family, because I have a huge family. It was outdoors, at Phalen Lake, an incredibly well-used lake that draws lots of Hmong folk and others. We had a Lutheran ceremony and then a Hmong hand-tying ceremony. Aaron and I wore Hmong clothes for the Lutheran ceremony and then changed; Aaron wore a suit and I wore a Thai wedding dress (as a tribute to my girlhood dreams of Num Sornram Teppitak). I cried through most of the day, a combination of allergies to the tiger lilies in my bouquet and sadness—for I was a Hmong woman and I understood marriage, no matter how relaxed the terms, how outside the structure of Hmong life it would be, to be a departure . . . from girlhood, from the home of my mother and my father, and the everyday experiences of my brothers and sisters.

———

I have been married to Aaron for the last three years. My understanding of race has changed significantly in our time together. While I used to experience racism daily with my family, it is rarer now with a white man beside me. It takes me by surprise when it happens.

Two years ago, Aaron and I decided we would watch a Minnesota Vikings game at Memory Lanes, a bowling alley and bar with large televisions a few blocks from our house. Aaron's father was to join us. When we got to the place, my father-in-law was already there at a table. We had a nice dinner, burgers and fries. Aaron and his father drank beer. I had a mug of hot water. All around us there were white folk, but many of the places we go in these cities—unless identifiably ethnic like a pho restaurant on University Avenue or a public venue like a zoo, a park, or a mall—are fairly white. Aaron's father left shortly after dinner. Aaron and I were going to stay and finish the game.

I needed to pee.

There was no one in the bathroom. There was only one toilet stall. I went in. As I was sitting there, I heard the door open and conversation ensue. I could tell that there was a small line. I flushed the toilet and opened the stall's door. There were two white women. I smiled. They did not smile back. They looked me up and down. They snickered and then sneered, looked at each other, and walked out.

It happened so fast. I was caught in their stares. I couldn't move. It took the swinging of the door behind them to free me. At the sink, I dispensed soap into my hands, turned on the water, and looked at myself in the mirror. My black hair was pulled back in a ponytail. I was in sweats, comfortable, football-watching gear. My vision blurred. I felt heat erupting inside and my throat thickening, could taste the tears welling up. I rushed. I washed my hands, dried them, and exited the bathroom. I walked to Aaron and our small table, cleared of food now, holding only our cups.

The women were in a booth by the wall. There was a bigger group, perhaps five or six people. I couldn't make out what they said, but the women looked at me. I felt exposed. I didn't want them to see me cry.

Aaron said, "What's wrong?"

I said, "We have to go. I don't want to cry in here."

As I said the words, the tears fell. I couldn't hold back. I hadn't expected the racism. I had gone through two years of living in relative quiet with Aaron by my side. Yes, my mother and father, brothers and sisters, experienced it. Yes, I took on racism as part of the work I have to do in the world when I give talks and write. But no, I had not expected the encounter in the bathroom. I grabbed my jacket, my hat, my mittens, and Aaron followed me out into the dark night, the quiet street.

We walked in silence for a while. I took deep breaths of the cold autumn air. When I could, I told Aaron what happened. He didn't know how to react. He placed an arm around me. He was quiet.

His quiet made me cry some more. I felt alone. The incident had isolated me. I missed my mother and my father. I missed my brother and my sister. I kept thinking, if my brother Xue were with me, if I had told him what had happened, he would have stood up for me. How? I didn't know. He would have said, "Let it run down your back" or "Haters are gonna hate." Dawb, my older sister, my oldest friend, my support and my strength. I called her in Aaron's silence as we walked. She didn't pick up. Her husband did, another white guy, Phooj's dad. Bob said, "What were you doing going to a bar to watch a football game?" I could hear the frustration in his voice, not at me, but at what happened. He hated to admit that racism existed in the world. He was unsure of how to deal with it. But he loved the people he loved and loved them deeply and I was one of them and I could hear the pain in his voice, his inability to protect me from what had transpired. He said, "Don't cry. They are not worth your tears."

I said, "Okay."

It was not okay. I hung up the phone.

The night had grown colder. Aaron was quiet beside me. I could sense his loneliness next to mine. My anger grew. Here was the man I had married. He had nothing to say about how I had been treated, how wrong it was, how much pain it had caused me, no words to salve the hurt inside of me, no way of doing so. He had no right to be lonely when it was I who was clearly alone in that restroom, at that table. I pulled my jacket tight around me.

———

I have discovered that there is no satisfying resolution in the face of racism when the person you are with is white. I know that Aaron is saddened by these instances and that he sympathizes with me. The problem is that he has a hard time responding to them because he understands his own complicity in the system.

When Aaron and I visited his sister in Anchorage, Alaska, and we asked her to take us to a Hmong grocery store so that we could cook a Hmong meal for the family, she took us to a part of town that she rarely goes to because it is the "bad" side of town. In a room, on a bed, in their house on the "good" side of town, my heart breaks quietly because my spirit yearns to be where my people are—good or bad, good and bad, with all their challenges and complications.

On vacation with Aaron's mother and father in Vale, Colorado, my first vacation ever, the service people have dark hair like me. Each exchange with a person of color is an exchange of dollars. The conversation is about how much to tip. I look across the expanse of the resort and wonder where the people like me—men who aren't much taller than my father, women who walk with the same ache in their feet as my mother—where they go at night. In the large suite that Aaron's mother and father have given us, I cannot sleep. I toss and turn on the king-size bed against a reality that feels like a nightmare.

One of Aaron's nephews is on a waiting list for a school his brother attends. While sibling preference is something that the school considers, they have an obligation to the children in the neighborhood. Aaron's sister and brother-in-law do not want to separate their sons. They don't want to send the one to a nearby school because it is by a trailer park and "those parents are not active." They schedule a meeting with the administration. They are both white and they are both lawyers and the meeting goes well: their child is accepted.

Aaron's mother and father share the story with us over dinner. Aaron is angry because he feels that more than any educational program, his nephews need "diversity" and exposure to difference. By difference, he means race and class. I don't say anything but I know it is white privilege at work that opens up a place for the nephew. I know it is class at work. I know there are huge overlaps.

One of Aaron's younger relatives has a long history of "messing" with other kids at school. He is medicated for ADHD. He has never been expelled. Each time there is a problem, his parents are called in and a new plan to help him is set in motion. Over the dinner table, Aaron's mother and father wonder if he is too smart for the classroom work and thus bored, they muse over whether he has gotten sufficient sleep or not and if that might be the cause of his actions, they suggest that it is the teachers and the strictness of the classroom protocol that won't allow for his creative energies to grow. I know how many boys of color his age are expelled for less than a push or a punch at another kid every day in Minneapolis and St. Paul—and across this very large nation of ours. I know how many of these young men will be imprisoned one day and how they will disappear from the landscape of America.

Race has become increasingly complicated since I married a white man and entered a white family. I see on a much more intimate level how the system works and where it gains its power—love. People protect those they love. The problem in an interracial marriage is that the people we love shift. We have to ask ourselves whether and how we will protect them. How do I protect Aaron? How do I protect myself? My family? His?

———

How do I protect Phooj?

Phooj is two and a half years old. We are at a busy Hmong grocery store on Maryland Avenue on St. Paul's East Side. We are waiting in line at the deli. He is sitting in the cart, dangling his red Power Ranger sneakers, holding tight to a mango-flavored jelly drink from Japan, marveling at the packages of sticky rice sausage, purple taro buns, and white steam rolls neatly organized on a food-warming island beside us. I can smell the pungent scent of fish sauce and tamarind, hear the thumping of a wooden pestle into a clay mortar, imagine the sweet and sour, tangy spiciness of Lao-style papaya salad. Two young Hmong men are behind us.

I hear one say to the other, "Look at the boy."

I ignore them. I ask Phooj what he wants from the deli.

He tells me in Hmong, "*Kuv yuav noj nabvam.*"

The young men marvel out loud, "Wow. He knows how to speak Hmong!"

I turn to them. I say, "Yes, he does."

The shorter one says, "He's half Meka."

Before I can answer, Phooj says to me, "I'm not half. I'm like you, Auntie Kalia. I'm Hmong. Just like you."

He scowls at the young men. They laugh at him. They think he is adorable. He does not think the same of them.

I say, "It's okay, Phooj."

The taller one says, "He is super cute. I can't believe he speaks Hmong. Lots of Hmong kids can't even speak the language like that."

I say, "Yes, he speaks Hmong well. His mom is Hmong."

Phooj is hurt. I can see it on his expressive face. His thin brows, like his mother's, are furrowed in a cross between confusion and pain.

He says in a whisper, "I am Hmong, too."

THE PRICE WE PAY

How Race and Gender Identity Converge

Andrea Jenkins

Andrea Jenkins, Intermedia Arts board chair and Bush Fellow, is a writer, performer, educator, and activist. A locally and nationally recognized poet, she has earned many awards, fellowships, and commissions. She is an oral historian at the Tretter Collection at the University of Minnesota Archives.

We dreamed you Black, in your badness
Made you up out of poems, and lies and words to live by
And we ourselves was dreamed, most likely by some slaves
Whenever they got a little space to climb into their heads and
*   be free*
So when they closed their eyes, what did they see?
They saw you . . . they saw me . . .

—Sekou Sundiata, "Longstoryshort"

There are no baby pictures of me, at least none that I have ever seen. I asked my mother about this once, and she began to cry, saying, "We were so poor, your dad and I were young, Black, and ignorant. We just didn't have the resources to take pictures of you two. There were no cell phones or digital cameras, and we couldn't afford to go to a photographer."

Poverty

I grew up in Chicago, Illinois; I was born in Cook County Hospital, in the heart of the West Side. My neighborhood, North Lawndale, is the same neighborhood that Ta-Nehisi Coates discusses in his groundbreaking 2014 article in the *Atlantic*, "The Case for Reparations":

> North Lawndale had long been a predominantly Jewish neighborhood, but a handful of middle-class African Americans had lived there starting in the '40s. The community was anchored by the sprawling Sears, Roebuck headquarters. North Lawndale's Jewish People's Institute actively encouraged blacks to move into the neighborhood, seeking to make it a "pilot community for interracial living." In the battle for integration then being fought around the country, North Lawndale seemed to offer promising terrain. But out in the tall grass, highwaymen, nefarious as any Clarksdale kleptocrat, were lying in wait.[1]

In 1961, the year I was born, this neighborhood began to change.

According to the most recent statistics, North Lawndale is now on the wrong end of virtually every socioeconomic indicator. In 1930 its population was 112,000. Today it is 36,000. The halcyon-days talk of "interracial living" is dead. The neighborhood is 92 percent Black. Its homicide rate is 45 per 100,000—triple the rate of the city as a whole. The infant mortality rate is 14 per 1,000—more than twice the national average. Forty-three percent of the people in North Lawndale live below the poverty line—double Chicago's overall rate. Forty-five percent of all households are on food stamps—nearly three times the rate of the city at large. Sears, Roebuck left the neighborhood in 1987, taking 1,800 jobs with it. Kids in North Lawndale need not be confused about their prospects: Cook County's Juvenile Temporary Detention Center sits directly adjacent to the neighborhood.

---

[1] Ta-Nehisi Coates, "The Case for Reparations," *The Atlantic* (June 2014): 57, www.theatlantic.com/magazine/archive/2014/06/the-case-for-reparations/361631/.

North Lawndale is an extreme portrait of the trends that ail Black Chicago. Such is the magnitude of these ailments that it can be said that Blacks and whites do not inhabit the same city. The average per capita income of Chicago's white neighborhoods is almost three times that of its Black neighborhoods. When Harvard sociologist Robert J. Sampson examined incarceration rates in Chicago in his 2012 book, *Great American City*, he found that a Black neighborhood with one of the highest incarceration rates (West Garfield Park) had a rate more than forty times that of the white neighborhood with the highest rate (Clearing). "This is a staggering differential, even for community-level comparisons," Sampson writes. "A difference of kind, not degree."[2]

In the late sixties and seventies, the gangs began to take over the drug trade, primarily heroin. The intergenerational effects of historical trauma from slavery, legislative oppression through Jim Crow laws, and intimidation, outright violence, and murder create a toxic environment for any child growing into their own.

In first grade, we were bused to Smyser Elementary, a school in a very nice neighborhood of Chicago, and I was taking piano lessons. My teacher told my mother I was a very strong student and convinced her to pay two dollars per month so that I could continue. My mother agreed but knew it would be almost impossible for her to come up with funds every month. And many months she didn't, but the teacher still let me go to class. I remember one month the students' envelope came up missing and the teacher thought I took it. She wrote a note for me to take home, telling my mom of her suspicions, and my mother wrote back that she indeed paid that month.

But that wasn't my biggest disappointment that year. You see, it was 1968, the year Martin Luther King, Jr., was assassinated, and riots broke out all over America. On April 4 all the Black kids were sent home early, and we never returned to that school again.

---

[2] As quoted in Coates, "The Case for Reparations," 59.

Who knows if I would have had a career at the piano? I had a shot, but racism and bigotry cost me that opportunity.

The Peculiar Price

Despite these early challenges and systemic oppressions, I was a good student; I went to the number-one-rated public high school in Chicago: Lindblom Technical High School. Lindblom was a rigorous college preparatory school, and about 80 percent of my classmates went on to college. I applied to the College of Liberal Arts (CLA) at the University of Minnesota. I was conditionally accepted *if* I attended their Summer Institute for "minority" students (I dislike that term and prefer students of color or Black, but that was the language in 1979), and instead of being in CLA, they would admit me to General College (GC), which was for remedial students. Even though my grades, ACT scores, and other qualifications were on par with the broader student population, GC was my only choice.

I actually surprised myself during my first year, doing much better than even I expected, but in year two, my grades began to suffer. The stereotyping that placed me in an inferior position created a self-fulfilling prophecy, a vicious cycle of low expectations and low achievement. Money, housing, and my gender identity became larger issues, and by the end of my sophomore year, I had to leave the university.

Yes, I said my gender identity. I cannot discuss racism without the intersection of my Transgender status. You see, once upon a time I was a picture-perfect model of an African American man. Tall, dark, handsome. I was well respected in most circles, dated beautiful women, and even belonged to a secret brotherhood. I played with balls: basketballs, footballs, volleyballs, and tennis balls; yes, I was one of those guys who constantly scratched my balls, even in public. I was all testosterone, all the time.

Over time I came to grips with my true internal feelings. I had feelings of confusion related to having an obviously male body and what I call a female psyche. By this time, it was crying time. One time I fucked three different women all in the same day. True story. Morning time, noontime, nighttime. By this time I was overcompensating for what I thought made men *men*. You know what I mean? I was trying to prove, to myself and others, that I had what it took. And what in fact is it that makes the man? Is it taking responsibility for one's family, one's community?

Can a man shed tears? Can a Black man live free in a racist America? And what constitutes the attributes of a woman? Where is that line that distinguishes the differences between the genders?

The late poet and spoken word artist Sekou Sundiata said, "I once married a woman who had her back turned." Women bleed, they make babies, bake bread—Black women sit on stoops all over this country and braid the hair of young gangbangers. They are the backbone of the community; *they create a way out of no way.*

But I will never make babies, never. Am I still a woman? Blood will never escape from between my legs unless I cut myself shaving in the shower. Am I still a woman? And yet the Creator imbued me with the heart of a woman, a woman-spirit if you will. This has enabled me to cross the demarcation of genital-based gender and explore the state of in-between-ness.

This combination of being African American and Transgender deeply impacts the price I pay to live in this society. It was the main reason I left school. You see, one day my roommate came home and found me having sex with an older white man. He was furious—he was Black and couldn't imagine continuing to live with a "fag." He kicked me out, leaving me with no resources and nowhere to go but back home to Chicago. He didn't know that I wasn't gay, but rather Transgender. There was no way I was able to admit that to anyone, not even myself. That wouldn't come for quite some time. After marriage, a beautiful daughter, a bitter divorce, and several failed relationships, I was finally able to come to grips with my reality and begin to live authentically with myself and others.

So what has this cost me as a Transgender Woman of Color?

eighteen

eighteen

18 hours since her last meal, her head is spinning with
    desperation,
hyper-sexualized body looks good, but the five o'clock
    shadow is nine hours over
the limit and her wig is beginning to look matted

she was 18 when she left home, college was life on the
    streets
the school day was long, seemed like it never ended,
    many nights spent on
sticky tricks' sofas, days spent as a social activist,
    marching, lobbying, organizing

18 Trans women of color gathering for an outpouring
    of self love,
Laverne Cox said that "loving a Trans woman of color
    is a revolutionary act"
sistas are doing it for themselves . . .

walking the streets of Bangkok, Thailand, 18 hours
    before a life-altering
surgery, body didn't evolve the way she dreamed of in
    her tiny bed, inside
a shared bedroom that proved to be unsafe

her mind flashed back to that birth certificate, assigned
    male at birth
socialized in a patriarchal world, yet unable to fully
    relate to the constant
challenge of trying to live her truth in an upside-down
    reality

18 times she threw out all of her women's clothing,
    known in the community
as the purge, ridding oneself of all the reminders of the
    transgression she's
contemplated by the day, annually, for as long as she
    can remember

doctors prescribe birth control pills for women for
    approximately 18 days a month, but
some Trans women take estrogen every day, the
    desired effects never really come though,
still she remains faithful to the goddess

18 candles on Transgender Day of Remembrance,
    18 Trans women of color murdered
and not always by those who hate them, but by men
    who have made love and shared
love with them, but want to keep these secrets in the
    dark

s/o to 18 trans sistas out there doing the damn thang,
CHERNO BIKO, LOURDES ASHLEY HUNTER, ARIANNA
    LINT, CECILIA CHUNG,
VALERIE SPENCER, ASHLEY LOVE, ANGELICA ROSS,

ARYKAH CARTER, MONICA ROBERTS, MISS MAJOR!,
    JANET MOCK, LAVERNE COX,
TRACEE MCDANIEL, REINA GOSSETT, CECE MCDONALD,
PARADISE LASHAY, REHEMA MERTINEZ, JUNE REMUS

it's been 18 years since this journey began, a long way
    from the days of fear and
loathing, and although her life might seem charmed to
    outsiders, she knows that her

Trans brothers and sisters are struggling out there, so
    she tells their story

everywhere she's invited, the Mayo Clinic, the Program
    in Human Sexuality, All Gender Health Seminars,
The Women's Foundation, Ramsey County, the Human
    Rights Campaign Dinner,
The Centers for Disease Control, Macalester College,
    the Arcus Foundation,

The University of Minnesota Medical School, Hamline
    University, the Minnesota Transgender Health
    Coalition,
Metropolitan State University, TransOhio,
The Minneapolis Urban League,

HRSA (Health Resources and Services Administration),
    the Task Force Creating Change Conference, and
    everywhere
else she goes, visibility is key to changing
the narrative that shapes this poem

the tables are rapidly turning, attention is being paid,
    TIME Magazine put a Trans
woman of color on the cover and said the Transgender
    Movement was at the "Tipping Point:
America's Next Civil Rights Frontier," and while that's
    true

18 Trans women of color will likely be arrested tonight,
    processed and locked
up with the male population or placed in solitary for
    their own protection,
becoming more victims of the prison industrial
    complex

that thrives on poor, black bodies, to fuel the
    monetization of black labor,
for corporate interests, how does she get through this
    madness? She remembers
those 18 hours of hunger, those 18 years of struggle,
    the 18 Trans sistas

showing each other love, she remembers the 18 hours
    strolling around Bangkok,
the 18 times she purged, and the 18 lives honored on
    TDOR, the 18 different places where she's shared
    their story of
brilliance, resilience, and beauty

Reparations

In his article, "The Case for Reparations," Ta-Nehisi Coates also
states:

> The early American economy was built on slave labor. The
> Capitol and the White House were built by slaves. Presi-
> dent James K. Polk traded slaves from the Oval Office.
> The laments about "black pathology," the criticism of
> black family structures by pundits and intellectuals, ring
> hollow in a country whose existence was predicated on
> the torture of black fathers, on the rape of black moth-
> ers, on the sale of black children. An honest assessment
> of America's relationship to the black family reveals the
> country to be not its nurturer but its destroyer.
>   And this destruction did not end with slavery. Dis-
> criminatory laws joined the equal burden of citizenship
> to unequal distribution of its bounty. These laws reached
> their apex in the mid-20th century, when the federal
> government—through housing policies—engineered the
> wealth gap, which remains with us to this day. When we

think of white supremacy, we picture Colored Only signs,
but we should picture pirate flags.[3]

This is the historical trauma that I carry with me on a daily
basis. I can interact with white people because I understand that
it is not the individual but rather the system of white supremacy that continues to hold us back. The thing is, however, that
the systems are created, perpetuated, and sustained by individuals. And there are people who benefit from this centuries-long
upside-down reality that renders Black folks victims of the con-
tinual plundering perpetrated by this system. And only *people* can
work to overcome these inequities in our society.

I suppose that other contributors to this dialogue can tell you
that Black people pay more for cars and houses than the broader
population. There is documentation that in Black communities
the food at the grocery store costs more and is of lesser quality
than food offered in the suburbs. All you have to do is turn on the
television and find that being Black can cost you your life, especially for Black men. Check for Tamir Rice, Trayvon Martin, Mike
Brown, Walter Scott, Freddie Gray, Eric Harris, or Eric Garner,
who was killed by a New York City police officer while pleading
for his life on video, saying, "I can't breathe."

Blacks in America are the only group of people that have been
violently, legislatively, and legally disaffected by the very system
that we built. Yet we continue to pay our fair share of taxes and
contributions. We, Black Americans, continue to move this grand
social experiment called America closer to one of the best models
of democracy in the world.

But this country also fears Black America; non-Blacks worry
that if we actually had equal opportunity in this society that we
Black Americans just might achieve more than they could imagine. They fear that we might begin to do the things to them that
have been done to us. I don't how that would actually play out,
but I know that it needs to happen.

---

[3] Coates, "The Case for Reparations," 59.

But if you're this far into this essay, you know that I—a Black American transwoman—started out with a significant deficit in life and suffered many losses and indignities along the way. I have come to understand that because of transphobia and racism I will only get so far in life, am only expected to achieve so much. It takes every ounce of strength I have to get up and face the world every day. Real talk.

This is the same scenario for all African Americans in this country; we have been deeply injured as a community. Collectively we experience the trauma of higher rates of controllable disease and die of them at higher rates; our life-spans tend to be shorter, based on a number of environmental factors including stress, poor diet, and discrimination. Unemployment rates are over double that in the broader community, and our public schools are tragically failing.

Coates, in his strong argument for reparations, states, "What I'm talking about is more than recompense for past injustices—more than a handout, a payoff, hush money, or a reluctant bribe. What I'm talking about is a national reckoning that would lead to spiritual renewal. Reparations would mean the end of scarfing hot dogs on the Fourth of July while denying the facts of our heritage. Reparations would mean the end of yelling 'patriotism' while waving a Confederate flag. Reparations would mean a revolution of the American consciousness, a reconciling of our self-image as the great democratizer with the facts of our history."[4]

On time: 1. at an appointed time 2. for or by payment by installments

And so now we come to the end of this moment in time. This journey through my life is not disconnected from the world around me. Barack Obama is the president of the United States, in the last months of his second term. Obama's former minister, the Rev. Jeremiah Wright, was crucified in the media for his comments

---

[4] Coates, "The Case for Reparations," 59.

condemning America's racist actions toward its citizens of all races. Unscrupulous mortgage brokers have undermined the entire world economy mainly by preying on low-income African Americans through the use of subprime mortgages. In many ways, however, it feels like the situation is worse now than before Obama was elected. It is certainly no better for Black people in Minnesota. In an online article for *24/7 Wall Street*, Minnesota is listed as the second-worst state for Black Americans.

MINNESOTA

- Black residents: 5.4%
- Black homeownership rate: 25.7% (5th lowest)
- Black incarceration rate: 2,321 per 100,000 people (22nd lowest)
- Black unemployment rate: 15.0% (tied-11th lowest)
- Unemployment rate, all people: 4.9% (9th lowest)

A typical black household in Minnesota earned less than half the median income of white households in 2013, well below the 62.3% nationwide. Low incomes among the black population are likely due in part to a high unemployment rate. While 15% of black workers in the state were unemployed in 2013, fewer than 5% of the total workforce did not have a job, a gap nearly twice as large as the national gap. High unemployment rates tend to lead to higher rates of people without health insurance, as a majority of Americans receive health insurance through their employers. While only 6.9% of white residents did not have health insurance in 2013, nearly 33% of blacks were uninsured. Additionally, black Minnesotan households were three times less likely than white households to own their homes, a rate nearly twice as high as the rest of the nation. Across the country, black Americans were also more likely to be disenfranchised as a result of the criminal justice system. In 2013, more than 7% of Minne-

sota's black population was barred from voting as a result
of felony convictions or imprisonment.

A Chinese proverb insists, "May you live in interesting times."
Indeed we do, but like the words to the song sung by the late,
great Sam Cooke, "I was born by the river, and just like that river,
I been running ever since. It's been a long, long time coming, but
I know a change gon' come, oh yes it will."

SONGLINES FOR FUTURE CULTUREWALKERS

(Betty) White (Crocker) Bank Take Little (House on the Prairie) Bank

Robert Farid Karimi

Robert Farid Karimi is an award-winning interdisciplinary play-wright, experience designer, and poet whose interactive performances feed audiences a mixed bowl of humor, pop culture, and personal history. A National Poetry Slam Champion, he has appeared in a variety of eclectic venues worldwide. His work has been published and recorded internationally.

These new people ["who have been brought up hopelessly, tragically, deceitfully, to believe that they are white"] are, like us, a modern invention. But unlike us, their new name has no real meaning divorced from the machinery of criminal power. The new people were something else before they were white— Catholic, Corsican, Welsh, Mennonite, Jewish—and if all our national hopes have any fulfillment, then they will have to be something else again.

—Ta-Nehisi Coates, *Between the World and Me*

I drop the phonograph needle onto the vinyl, a melody of your choosing plays—an Icelandic rock band, or Iowan Muslim hip-hop, or perhaps, just because, funk from a seventy-year-old grandpa who lives outside Minneapolis; he has the largest fingers thumpin' and pluckin' the bass with delicious mmhm that makes your body move. This is your Minnesota soundtrack. To give you that Minnesota Public Radio backdrop. *Watch out! One musical choice may get you accused of being white.*

I hold a white card with the word "WHITE" in black letters, hold it for 10 seconds. Replace it with another large card: black, with white letters: "BLACK." Then a brown one, with white letters: "BROWN." I replace that with a "RED" one, then a "YELLOW." Then "MATCH THE CARDS TO THE FOLLOWING CITIES." First: "Pine Ridge, SD." "Oakland," "Los Angeles," "Minneapolis." For fun: "Lima, Peru."

I sip my tea. You watch my sexy lips move, and hear me say:

When I decided to move to Minnesota from California, I clenched my body because everyone said I had to brave the . . . *white people.*

"Oh my god," a friend rolled his eyes, "so many! You are going to the land of Garrison Keillor and boring public radio! At least they're liberal. It's not Texas."

Everyone had an opinion of what my life would be like. "Think Fargo." "You know, the people who go on missions to Guatemala."

Fair or not fair, I began to realize that Minnesota means white for America. Not southern redneck white, but northern white: "People are cold," one friend warned. "Imagine a whole place where no one hugs and everyone stays to themselves. Especially because you didn't go to high school with them."

———

Pop culture placed the first images of Minnesota in my head. Mary Tyler Moore worked in Minneapolis. It's the place where Betty White's character claimed origin. Betty Crocker, who taught my Central American mother how to cook like a United Statesian, lived in Minnesota. And to get my childhood imaginative dreamland simmering before bedtime, my mother read tales of Minnesota and beyond from *Little House on the Prairie.* Minnesota: land of Laura Ingalls Wilder running down the hills with huge smiles of possibility.

Happy people everywhere! So I thought when I landed in West St. Paul, years before I moved to the Twin Cities, even the Mexicans seemed happy. Joyous African American men strolled arm in arm with women who appeared European. And the Shakopee

Mdewakanton Sioux who owned the casino with the rooftop laser light show (the first Native casino I saw in my life!) walked around with so much joy. Ah, this is so Nice. Minnesota, a Rodgers and Hammerstein musical. I felt like Bjork in the movie *Dancer in the Dark*, whose factory character daydreamed of all her fellow workers singing and dancing in harmony. My friends, so silly, so silly.

———

A Filipino filmmaking friend visited me one day, he remarked, "Minneapolis is the place our parents thought they were immigrating to with blond, blue-eyed people and open spaces and nice neighborhoods. Instead they got stuck (in the San Francisco Bay Area) with living in diverse neighborhoods with no white people."

———

As a child, I never used the word white. We said, "gringos." Well, at least everyone on my mom's side, the Guatemalans, did. My dad, from Iran, used the word at certain times for comedic effect. Gringos were "Americans" from the United States, greedy, selfish imbeciles, those who did not care about others. My family called me a gringo when I did something callous, a childhood jab in the playgrounds of Guatemala.

"Oye! Gringo! Gringo!"

I protested. The word felt best suited for the bully in my elementary classroom who beat up people if they were smaller, foreign, or didn't help him with his homework.

———

I stop the record.

I glare at you, straight up, with my smoldering hazel eyes, say:

When I first encountered midwestern poets of my generation, my West Coast friends and I always remarked on how angry they were about the White Man. Their poems always had a rage unique to their experience. Outnumbered by the "White Man" here in Minnesota and other places, these writers spoke loudly and fiercely to counterbalance their previous silence. We West Coasters didn't understand. We went to schools surrounded by Asians, Latinos, African Americans, and very few people who called themselves white. We thought the midwesterners were blinded by whiteness. They used the words "People of Color." White this or white that. Whitey as enemy was everywhere. In a workshop I led at the Loft, a poet, a Korean adoptee, talked about her rage about her white adoptive parents. I, the West Coaster, was confused. Why is everyone smiling on the outside? Isn't this the home of the American Dream and Ma and Pa? My musical, falling apart, became dissonant and discordant.

I drop the needle, again.

———————

In 2009, the Race exhibit at the St. Paul Science Museum appeared. The idea of a science museum displaying race evokes images of Filipinos on display at the 1904 World's Fair and eugenics. The 2009 exhibit amplified how people use race to objectify. The magnified objectivity of a museum space made the exhibit seem at best absurd, at worst hypocritical.

Yet here I stood in the museum collaborating with St. Paul's premiere African American theater company on a performance/educational interactive experience that I imagined would challenge people, make them uncomfortable, and create the dialogue I felt the Race exhibit lacked.

It was here, in these rehearsals, that an African American man said, "You're white. Talk about your experience as a white man."

Whoa! I looked myself over. Had I just won the lottery? Had the lack of sun from being this far north of the Mason-Dixon Line changed my shade? Were his words a sly slur? I did not know what to do. Do I explain that I am Iranian and Guatemalan and stop the rehearsal, or do I just nod, say I am not white, and move on? I bit my tongue, wanting to keep my job, and wrote a piece for the performance about what simmered inside me.

I pass.

It wasn't until I moved to Minneapolis
that someone said,

"You're white. At least you can pass."

Usually people can't tell what I am, so when I say that
I am half Iranian and half Guatemalan, they usually
respond with [Karimi mouths words] "Damn!"

Here in Minnesota . . . I, Robert Farid Karimi, can pass
for being a white man?

In the U.S., I have been called half breed.

In Mexico, and most of Latin America, I am an Arabe.

When I was in France, I was called mélange because no
one would accept I was an American.

I pass?

When I pass through customs, I always get the extra
search after they look at my passport. They see the
face, the facial hair, the Farid, the Karimi (which
are not Scandinavian names, thank you very much),
and stop and ask if I know the capital of North
Dakota, where I was born, and what is my business
in this country? What should I say?

In the discussion of race in the country, I am passed, up.

Still stuck in a black and white paradigm
that sees race as a tug of war of two extremes,

where other cultures are not allowed to play
and mixed race isn't even invited to the party.

I step up to be a part of the diversity feast,
but I am not asked to the table,
still stuck in the kiddy corner of the cultural discussion.

I can pass, though.

Passing used to mean
"Moving on Up
to a De-lux apart-
ment in the Skyy . . ."
getting out of whatever oppression held a person down:

Jim Crow, Juan Crow,
race was never
on the down low,

used to Yellow-star
Pink-triangle people
into proper nouns of Prejudice.

Passing meant people
thought a person's identity
was just a coat, not a shackle,
as if the passer had the key
to run free from oppression.

When someone now says I, Robert Farid Karimi, can
     pass, it means:

Good immigrant, stay over there. You can pass.

Oh, you can pass.

You can pass for smart Asian,
you can pass for lackin' melanin,

you can pass
knowing who you are
where you came from,
you can pass,
just be American,
pass up the stories from your grandparents, your
    family,
you can pass.

But then
who would I be
if I did?
If I became that person
who just removed
my history, my grandparents,
my ancestry
off like a coat
and poured blood on
it and told my parents
that it died in a horrible accident?
Who would I be if
I pushed away
all the cultures that made me
Iranian Guatemalan Italian Filipino Latino
African, American, LGBT, hip-hop, disco, House
punk rock, televi-sion
on and on and on . . . just to be considered black or
    white.

Just so I can pass.
With the impending war in Iran, will I pass?
If they ask me, which side am I on, will I pass?

Next time someone says I can pass
I will ask them:
what if you could pass?
Would you want to
be anything you wanted to be
when someone takes your liberty?
A shapeshifter?
A cultural chameleon?

Here's your I-pass. It can be your iPass. It's the 21st
    Century.

Because if it is that simple to pass,
then everyone should be able to do it.

[Karimi passes I-passes to audience]

Here, take yours.

Write down what you pass for,
anytime you need it.
You never know.

―――――

Afterward, my body still reverberated from the experience. To be
called "white" in a room of mostly African Americans assumes I
have power and agency, and that I am not considered part of the
family. This may not have been the person's intent, but I started
to learn that Minnesota had an unspoken friction, and I had been
duped. No Little House for me.

―――――

The record skips, while it does I read from a crumpled piece of
paper:

Minneapolis

There are no white people on the bus today. At least no one who would claim to be white. Not saying, there is no one on the bus that would consider to be considered white. To be able to walk in to the bank white. To smile at the police officer checking bus passes, as white. To sit in the back of the bus, white. Or, perhaps, walk off the bus, two stops before their intended destination, white, powerful, to grab a drink, just a human being, bearded with possibilities.

When I first moved to Minnesota, most folks didn't say they were white. They proclaimed their heritage. Germans, Swedes, Norwegians, French. Strange, I thought. When did they become white? Maybe winter changes people into colors. I waited to see.

All this white talk tires me. Whiteness implies essentialism, and mélanges, like me, usually get relegated to the backseat during that conversation. Think about it: when do you use the word "white" with the word "people"? I hear it always in reference to power and powerlessness. Manifest Destiny. Oppression. Big Bank take little bank, or in this case: White Bank take little bank.

When people use color to identify themselves, in general they want me to join their cause, their club, or buy their Amway product. It omits our heritage, our story.

This isn't a call for post-racialness. Whiteness excludes me or wants to consume me. Why should I give it so much power?

Let's change the record. Something that makes us move. Yes!

This experience of passing made me hyperaware of race. After six months of living in Minnesota, I started to get a weird feeling.

Every time I encountered someone who appeared to be non-white or non-Minnesotan, my body sonically buzzed, like Aquaman, and I hoped our telepathy would connect us. "We're the same, my people!" ran through my head, and I, like a magnet, would run toward them. I never stalked anyone. Okay maybe once, when I thought this dude was Iranian and Mexican, but only then. I swear.

In the San Francisco Bay Area or Chicago, I never had this feeling. I knew different cultural communities don't just like each other because we are from the same geographic place or we don't automatically consider ourselves some rainbow label like "People of Color." Yet, here in Minnesota, I became a fiend for anyone who could be familia, part of the cultural diversity I hungered for, someone who understood without explanation why my cultural heritage was not a terrorist state, or someone who would just give me a head nod saying, "I got you (Fellow Citizen of People of Color community)." I just wanted to be a part of "People of Color." I wanted to embrace my Brownness. Celebrate Black, Yellow, Red, and any other color someone told me they were. The people who invented White People had won. In Minnesota, I craved the heat of color.

———

Working with different members of the Hmong community the last seven years, I discovered that there are no words for my identities in their language. While working in the Hmong Elder Center in St. Paul, the elders just called me "mekas." White man, my Hmong co-facilitator told me as she laughed. That was my designation.

Here I was a gringo again. This time mekas became my trickster mask. I played the Fool to make people laugh or to get them to tell me a story. If I was a gringo/mekas, then I'd play the bumbling role. It made the elders laugh, but also got us trying to find a way for my identity to go beyond being just a mekas.

———

Then something happened. Just when I figured it all out, someone reminded me I did not pass. While Iraq War 2 continued in full bloom, someone brought me full circle. I was at a bar in Minneapolis. And my friend Jason had just met a tall handsome stranger. My girlfriend and I were dancing, laughing, and having fun. Trying to make a good impression so Jason could, you know. And this stranger, this stranger who is trying to hook it up with my friend Jason, says.

STRANGER
You know, you look like Saddam Hussein!

And I can see Jason mouthing, "Why did you do that?" And I'm cool. Then the tall handsome stranger, the one who's trying to hook it up with my friend Jason, says,

STRANGER
No really, you look like Saddam Hussein.

The young man would not stop calling me Saddam Hussein. No malice in his voice. More, "Oh My God! You look like a celebrity." He kept raising his voice to emphasize his amazement, but I could not get him to shut up. Yelling *Saddam Hussein* in a club? Why not yell out *Fire*? In one moment, I became danger, terrorist, outcast. I did not belong. Reminded I looked like the Enemy of the People at a dance club. And the one that killed Iranians during the war in the eighties no less. I said to myself, "Let it go, Karimi. Get over it." I couldn't. My dukes were up. I understood my poet friends. My anger rose. I did not want to share what I was feeling, afraid of the backlash.

Chapter 24: From the Land of Sky Blue Waters

In the Land of Sky Blue Waters, they teach their young
to listen, then coat the truth, so that it causes no harm.
Those, who have been there for years, know, when telling

a story, it is better to Hide than Weave. The Weavers lost land. The Weavers died. Yes, the Concealers, the ones who spoke in beautiful flirtatious flattering tones, became rich. They survived. The Weavers, those who did not give flowers when given flour, had their toes and eyes removed, and their tongues cut, so they couldn't pass on the stories that nourished their families from generations before.

———————

Minnesota had tapped into a rage I thought dormant. I came to Minnesota and discovered I am a person of color, am white, look like a terrorist, and because I never went to high school in Minnesota can only be considered an illegal immigrant of the Land of 10,000 Lakes. I was taut, waiting for the next slur, or another person to ask me which side of the war would I be on if we went to war with Iran.

Anger did not serve me. My idols have been comedians who transformed pain into laughter. I wanted my trickster soul back! Snow melts, I thought, there must be a way to melt "whiteness."

(P.O.W.)

White rappers enunciate their words very clearly.

Some Hmong (w)rappers (w)rap like some Filipino
    (w)rappers.
Some Hmong folks and some Filipino folks like
    Freestyle music.

I like lumpia.
    (Do I have to explain Lumpia is a Filipino Egg Roll?
    Just know that Asian (w)rappers (w)rap around
    vegetables, it doesn't mean they are vegetarian.)

There are many Filipinos in Saudi Arabia.
A boat with fertilizer was captured

with a lot of Filipinos on it
      by Somali pirates.

There was a lot of shit on that boat, but who treated
   who like shit?
        Would Hmong rappers and Filipino rappers
        treat each other like shit?

When does fertilizer become precious cargo?
When White rappers rap about it?

If I said I hate White rappers,
        would they finally write a rap about me?

I don't hate White (w)rappers.
I like the ones that enclose the chicken from the
   butcher.
           Those, I like.
              I know what they are.

I am not half bad.
Three-quarters. Seventy five cents.
        Thirty seven point five times   two cents.

These are mine—

If I tell White rappers that Hmong rappers and Filipino
   rappers are cool,
would they be put in a rap,
        so that the White rapper could be cool?

I am tired of White this, White that.
        I don't even call Wonder bread, White bread.
              It's Wonder!
              Wonder is wonder.
    The musical genius is not named Stevie White,

so why should it be
White bread?
Don't muddle it by calling it White Wonder.
Brett Favre. Beowulf. Bjork.
It's true. They are.

Cocaine. Freshly powdered sugar on french toast.
Yep.

It's not hard to see.
Even when I enunciate it clearly to you.
Why must I focus on one color when
There's Wonder everywhere?
It doesn't mean it's more powerful than awe.
(I mean, nothing's better than awe. Well, Wonder
is awe without fear.
And fear sucks,
so that makes Wonder   awesome.)

Maybe transcendence beats them all,
but Manifest Destiny or genocide is not necessary
in the name of Wonder.

Wonder now.
Ask.
Go ahead. Anything you want to know.
Why you don't use the word Hmong and
Filipino
in the same sentence?

Or where is the P.O.W. in this piece?
Perhaps it's Prisoners of Whiteness.
Maybe it's People of Wonder.

Or for you, political pundit of war—
John McCain!

Must every acronym be cleverly explained?
The answers fit to questions already.

Randomness has its own puzzle pieces
that fit perfectly,
you just don't know the answers.

Wonder doesn't need to dominate,
               neither does awe,
but when you've been in the presence of what you
    think is god,
                         that kicks ass.

No metaphors required to box in the experience,
it will probably lead to more questions,
             which is good.

Wonder.
yes, that's it.

Wonder.   nobody owns it.
Wonder.   and you don't have to enunciate.

Wonder rappers speak how they want to speak
so that you can keep   Wondering.

now, that's   powerful.

———————

In the end, I wonder:
If Prince were white, would he still be Purple?
If orange or aquamarine was part of People of Color, would
you claim it?
If the words "white people" were eliminated, would that bring
back all the people murdered by law enforcement?
If I watch *Orange is the New Black* on an old black and white

TV, would I eliminate injustice, inequity, and have time to make dinner for all of us so we could just listen to the end of the song?

If I.

If we.

I wonder.

───────

(The record is over. It's okay, you can change it. The groove continues. Dot. Dot. Dot.)

DISCOMFORT ZONE

Minnesota Born and Raised

Sherry Quan Lee

Sherry Quan Lee approaches writing as a community resource and as culturally based art of an ordinary everyday practical aesthetic. Her most recent book, *Love Imagined: a mixed race memoir*, was a 2015 Minnesota Book Award finalist.

Yes, I know that I don't look Black. Yes, I know that I don't look Chinese. What do I look like? I look like fear. I look like shame. I look like resignation. I look like hope. I am contemplative and quiet. I am irreverent and loud.

Anger. Shame. Trauma. I am Chinese. I am Black. I am feminist. I have been, I am still, sometimes angry. Anger for me is shame based. I have been, even before I was born, and I still sometimes feel, enveloped in shame. I have reacted by losing my temper, by hanging up the phone, by walking away, by running away. I do so less often now. I am aware of what and why and who push my proverbial buttons—people I like, people I love, people who are strangers. When I am reprimanded, when you are, apparently, right and I am wrong, I remember the girl who was never right, who was no one, and I panic. This cumulative knowledge and experience and remembrance of racism, of having to pretend I was something I was not, often emerges as trauma—a distress signal that causes me to react. Although I have intentionally distanced myself from less than a handful of friends, only a few have distanced themselves from me—unfortunately, the few include family members.

———

How not to write the same story? How not to repeat myself? How to write something new. To write something I haven't said before/haven't written before. How not to repeat what someone else has already said. What you have said. What needs to be said/to be written again. In different ways. In all ways.

I was born in 1948. My father is Chinese, born in China. My mother is "Negro," born in Minneapolis. I am *a little mixed up*; but culturally I was raised *white* in South Scandinavian Minneapolis. I've written this story before, many, many times. I am going to tell it again—but differently. Recalling from a third-person perspective how the girl, the woman I was, has now become the elder I am.

I am not in this particular story. I am hovering above, hunkering below, witnessing, remembering, remarking; invisible even as I approach you, reproach you.

———

She is looking at the girl I didn't know, the girl others didn't see; the woman I am now. It's the desire to be seen, to speak that has moved her forward, forced her to write. She writes from her center, South Minneapolis—east of Minnehaha Avenue, west of Chicago Avenue, south of Lake Street, north of Highway 62.

1953–1963. Her Chinese father and her Negro mother divorced when she was five, the youngest of four daughters, her mother pregnant with a son. She was shy. She cried. But she also prayed to God her father and wrote poetry. And she ate chow mein. Her father worked at the Nankin Café. Even after the divorce, the neighbor lady could drive downtown at midnight and get the leftover chow mein. Her mother would freeze the chow mein (this about the time that Swanson frozen TV dinners were popular). Despite growing up poor, she never went hungry for anything to eat. Yet she was hungry for something she couldn't then name.

Don't tell anyone you are Black (she didn't know she was), but if they ask, say you are Chinese. She could be a China doll, even a white Barbie; she didn't know any black beauties, but that's certainly not to say there weren't any. She attended Standish Elementary School, Folwell Junior High School, and Roosevelt High School.

1963–1966. Roosevelt High School. She remembers one Japanese teacher who taught math. One African American teacher who taught history. One Black football player. A sea of Swedes and Norwegians. She kept her head down, her mouth shut, her rose-colored makeup on. She attended the Lutheran church. She sang in the choir. She wasn't allowed to date (how was she to know how many parents wouldn't allow their son to embrace a mixed-race girl; how was she to know she was mixed race?) or go to football games in North Minneapolis (there might be a race riot; what was race? what was a riot?). She lived within the boundaries of the Standish neighborhood; she was safe, she was protected. Safe because she was white; her mother did not tell her otherwise—she didn't know she wasn't. Protected because her mother held her heart around her daughter and wouldn't let her go—anyplace, except school, and sometimes church. Yet lies and confinement have other consequences: shame, and a life-long search for truth—for love.

1966–1973. Her journey took her north of Lake Street to the University of Minnesota campus. She was a working girl, a college student, a late-coming-of-age girl who witnessed the city's diversity and shared an intimate space with girls from rural areas, new to the city, as well as with girls from the suburbs. It didn't take her long to learn who she was—the mixed-race girl with a Chinese father and a Negro mother—and who she wasn't—the white girl. Her eyes, her ears, her libido shattered her innocence.

A Black friend at college was the first to acknowledge she was Black—how did she know? (Most Black folk recognize her as Black; most Asian folk recognize her as Asian; most white folks don't have a clue.) She accepted her true identity with caution and fervor. Eventually the fervor took precedence. Everywhere she turned her life was about race. White boys wanting her but only momentarily because their parents didn't approve of them dating a girl who wasn't white; unless, like her husband, they lied. Yet nothing stopped her from continuing to look for love.

1973–1983. He, Bohemian and German, wouldn't tell his parents she was Black. Previously he was engaged to a Black woman and his parents threatened to disown him. She was tired of being shut down because of her race and told him to tell his parents whatever he wanted. She wasn't trying to pass; she was tired of trying to explain herself. He told them she was Polynesian (she didn't know what Polynesian was). They had two sons. Their sons had dark complexions. Her brown baby boys, one darker than the other and defined as Black by his friend in nursery school, presented her with a surreal knowledge that racism was alive and well in her immediate family.

Her husband, even after the children were born, refused to tell his parents she was Black and Chinese. When confronted, he said, *My parents love you, why tell them you are Black and not have them love you?* Her response was: divorce. She ran from the marriage and her little blue rambler with a two-car garage in the suburbs, in pursuit of a nebulous attainment of love that accepted herself and her sons for who they were.

———

Though education was hit-and-miss because searching for love was the priority, education was always a goal. Married, raising two children, and working full time, she attended community college. She searched for books she could identify with; finding none, she began to write her own story, poem after poem. Although one white professor told her it wasn't trendy to write about race, another embraced her story with much too much enthusiasm.

1983–1986. She completed an undergraduate college education that took twenty years to earn, due to detours—relationships, marriage, and children challenged her naïve and shallow knowledge of gender, sexuality, and race. She courageously flaunted her Chinese/Black female, often angry self and entered a stage wider and deeper than Minnesota had previously presented to her. She read her poetry, focused on her mixed racial identity, at various venues across the city, and her first chapbook, *A Little Mixed Up*, was published by Guild Press. *She didn't know then that anger was one response to shame—but, anger was also a motivation to move beyond the shame.*

1986–1998. Remarried and living in Minneapolis, south of the Standish neighborhood she grew up in, she experienced twelve years of mothering, being a wife, and knowing and sometimes desiring what was beyond a Tudor-style house in yet another mostly white neighborhood. She pursued a graduate degree and eventually fled what she thought was yet another constrictive and small and white experience. Although she went out of her way to claim she was Chinese and Black, everything around her was still white. Her husband was white; her neighbors were white. She was probably seen as white. Although she hoped her sons would embrace the diversity found in going to a city school, their friends were mostly white. Yet, the one time they were driving with other brown friends, the police stopped them. A few blocks from their home, police profiled the brown teenage boys who surely must have stolen that car from the suburbs to go joyriding in the city. The car was theirs; they were stopped in their own neighborhood and made a display of in their own backyard.

It wasn't so much the neighborhood as the shallowness of living within a family that didn't share her need to understand or embrace the complexity of who she was that kept her on the move. And it was a desire to more fully immerse herself into a life not defined by white middle-class privilege (not that she wanted to be poor).

1998–2009. In partnership with a Mexican woman, she thought she had finally realized *love*. Her love for women and her desire to be with someone intellectual, political, and not white was paradise, until it wasn't. Eventually, she realized that she and her partner, a caretaker and a narcissist, were like fire and ice, and the relationship smoldered until she disappeared. Yet, she continued to be vulnerable, taking risks to find love, only to add more stories to her repertoire.

2009–2015. Currently she has cornered herself in a suburb east of St. Paul that shelters her—not as she was sheltered in her childhood home in South Minneapolis from people of color, but from the vibrancy of Minneapolis, the boldness of its youth, the integrity and tenacity of those young and old making a difference, embracing each other and challenging each other to do the work in order for justice to be a given in the Twin Cities, in Minnesota, in America, in the world.

———

She chose her new home for financial reasons. Despite bad credit, she was able to buy a foreclosed condo. A one-level condo that will serve her well into retirement—affordable; she won't, she hopes, have to live in a publicly sponsored senior-citizen high-rise as her mother did. But she doesn't let geographical borders confine her. And she admits she hasn't explored what the culture of her new community might exude.

The work she does is writing, teaching, mentoring. She can do this work from wherever she resides. She is sixty-eight years old. Mother isolated her from the racism, the race riots—her own Negro family— in Minneapolis—from herself. She is no longer that little girl.

———

Since my book *Love Imagined: a mixed race memoir* was published, I have been in conversation with some of the Swedes and Norwegians I grew up with. I remember some things they don't; they remember things I don't; some of us remember the same things. I remember a church that didn't accept Black members, until a new minister arrived with adopted Black children. Some, surprisingly, remember they knew I was Black; others only remember me as Chinese. Truly, I don't know if anyone thought I was white. We remember mothers who smoked cigarettes. Baseball in the street. Cruisin' up and down Lake Street in a baby blue Mustang. We remember the corner grocery store, the donut shop, the Nile movie theater (Saturday matinees), the Friday night Sibley Park dances.

Most of my friends, including my siblings, went their own way after high school. For me, eighteen years living in the Standish neighborhood was the most stability I would ever experience. My journey since then has included over four dozen homes and various neighborhoods. It has been a chaotic lifetime of searching for myself in some of the most dangerous, beautiful, cluttered, questionable, and temporary places.

———

I know I am someone. I try desperately not to allow *Minnesota Nice*—for me, a patronizing pat on the back that signifies pity—or my friends or my family to make me feel small again, small like the little girl who was afraid, silent, and naïve and lived and breathed *whiteness* in the Miles Standish neighborhood of South Minneapolis.

I am a recovering Black/Chinese woman who grew up passing for white. Some days are easier than others, but some days I still feel the weight of living a lie. Not purposely, but passing in and out of boundaries that will always segregate all of whom I am. There will always be those pockets of whiteness where I blend in as white, but I know the truth. I attended an awe-inspiring Christmas tea at a friend's church. Each table set with festive china and centerpieces. But as much as I enjoyed the beauty and spirit of the space, something was lacking. It was an all-white congregation. Did anyone care if I wasn't white? Did anyone know I wasn't? Probably not. Did I feel welcomed? Yes. But I couldn't get past the feeling I didn't belong, I didn't want to belong, to belong I would have to filter out feelings of betrayal to the woman I have become. The woman who respects, desires, and is diversity. I am a woman of a generation of Minnesota baby boomers, most of whom were white, estranged from the diversity of today's Minnesotans.

I live in a discomfort zone. I can't separate the fact that culturally I grew up white, having little to no knowledge of Black or Asian cultures. Who am I to say when a white friend says, "but God loves everyone," that his naïve and simple understanding isn't any more profound than my reply, "but it's complicated"? Who is to say that because he's not protesting in the street, his small acts of kindness aren't just as meaningful? Yet, to not acknowledge and to not try to understand the trauma that racism has left many of us fighting—fighting for our lives and for those of our children—the trauma that many of us will spend a lifetime trying to understand, that many of us will spend a lifetime trying to obliterate—*thus missing out on a life that most with privilege can enjoy*—then naïveté is just that and, like Minnesota Nice, love that sees no color isn't love.

In 2010, Minnesota had 5,303,925 people—274,412 "Black or African American" and 214,234 "Asian"—more than ten thousand lakes, many rural towns and vibrant cities. I left Minnesota a few times—lived in Illinois, in Massachusetts, in Colorado, in Washington State—but I've always returned. Minnesota is my home, Minneapolis is where I was born, where I lived for eighteen years. Minneapolis/St. Paul, in the past, was mostly white, but now the Twin Cities are a population of many colors, many Chinese, many African American, many mixed race. Many who are doing the work, the exhaustive and brave work challenging and undoing racism and sexism, each in his/her/their own particular ways, especially the vulnerable work of telling their stories.

I live in Minnesota. I choose to live here. Cold and ice. Heat and humidity. Swedes and Norwegians. Irish. Italians. Polish people. African Americans: Somalis, Liberians, Nigerians. Asian Americans: Laotians, Chinese, Vietnamese, Hmong, Japanese, Koreans, East Indians. Native Americans. Migrants between Twin Cities, between neighborhoods. Communities of color meandering between lakes, between rivers, between freeways and highways; between cement walls. Minnesota is not the vibrant multidiverse East Coast or West Coast of the United States, but it is fast becoming a hub of diversity, a hub of activism, a hub of writers telling their stories. I have no desire to live elsewhere.

◇ PEOPLE LIKE US

David Lawrence Grant

David Lawrence Grant has written drama for the stage, film, and television, as well as fiction and memoir. He has written major reports on racial bias in the justice system for the Minnesota Supreme Court and on racial disparities in the health care system for the Minnesota legislature. He teaches screenwriting at Independent Filmmaker Project/Minnesota.

When the crack cocaine epidemic of the eighties and nineties finally caught up with Minneapolis, it caught up with a vengeance. During the long hot summers of '93–94, that epidemic created a staggering body count—enough to spark the moniker, "Murderapolis." This was just when the line between journalism and bread-and-circuses entertainment had rapidly begun to blur, but, still, the label was more than mere hype . . . because sure enough, during the mid-nineties, Minneapolis owned one of the highest per capita murder rates in the country.

Minneapolis, renowned for its clean streets, its clean, progressive politics, and its creative philanthropy, was suddenly famous for something else entirely, and it made both everyday citizens and civic boosters extremely uneasy.

There was the public hand-wringing and soul-searching that you would expect in the news stories and on the editorial pages. But there was a coolness to most of the coverage, too—a strange, unnerving sense, especially from the broadcast media, that the horror and trauma of it all was being observed from some sort of remove, as though all of this was actually happening someplace else.

Then, in 1995, a white woman named Anne Dunlap was found

dead in the trunk of her car in the parking lot of a South Minneapolis K-Mart. She was a young, pretty, successful suburbanite. Up until then, the growing list of dead putting the Murder in Murderapolis had all been poor and black or brown, residents of Minneapolis's most challenged neighborhoods in the near-south and near-north parts of town. But now, with Dunlap's grisly murder, the tone of the local media coverage suddenly shifted. Much of the change in tone was so subtle, it was hard for me to put my finger on it. Then, two or three days after she was found, I saw a report that brought stunning, painful clarity.

A white, female reporter walked the K-Mart parking lot at the end of her late-night dispatch on the Dunlap murder, making a little casual banter with the anchor back at the station—in the service of that thing they do sometimes to break through the coolness and distance that the medium itself creates . . . to show a little emotion, to declare a transitory "time out" and share what's meant to feel like an intimate, personal moment with us, the viewers.

The anchor asked her, "Well, there've been a lot of murders this year. Why do you think it is that *this* case has so completely captured our attention and stirred up our collective emotion the way it has?" There was a pregnant pause as the reporter looked into the camera. Her camera person, sensing that she was about to say something important and from the heart, zoomed in for a tight close-up on her face. "Well, I think it's hit us so hard because this time, it's someone like *us*." She and her anchor traded a soulful nod.

I nodded too—not because her words had resonated with me and moved me as she hoped they would move her audience, but because I understood something about the meaning of what she had just said, even if she herself did not. Her words had just made it crystal clear to me that I, and others who look like me, were not part of that *us* she'd imagined she was speaking to as she emoted into the microphone and the camera with such sincerity and urgency. I understood in a visceral way that as she surveyed her evening audience in her mind's eye, she didn't see me out there at all, only others who look like her anchor and herself.

In that moment, I could see with clarity why almost all the Murderapolis coverage I'd been reading and watching had felt so superficial and empty. It was because, in the minds of many of the people who were writing and delivering our area's news, the perpetrators and the victims at the center of these tragedies were, in some fundamental way, *not* people just like themselves . . . or their majority audience.

They were people of color, most of them, in a state whose long-standing self-image had always been that of a place where the overwhelming majority are of northern European heritage. They were persistently poor, most of them, in a place where there is a strong, mostly unspoken belief that if a family has been poor for an extended time—certainly for more than a generation—then there must be something terribly wrong with the fundamental character of the people in that family. It's a harsh judgment, but not a consciously hostile one. That's because the phenomenon we know as *Minnesota Nice* is much, much more than just a set of behaviors: it's an entire way of looking at and understanding the world that sits at the very heart of the culture here. And like any world view, it's just as full of rules—both spoken and unspoken—as it is full of truths, half-truths, lies, *damned* lies, and contradictions.

Deconstructing Minnesota Nice

People up here in our part of the country tend to be nice. *Very* nice. Anyone who visits for more than five minutes will quickly see that this niceness sits at the very pinnacle of the social values that Minnesotans prize the most. But *nice* is a word with shades of meaning and nuance that are as wide and as fathomless as the deep blue sea.

To be fair, Minnesota Nice, with many localized differences and cultural points of reference, applies to our entire region. But because the Twin Cities is the region's economic and cultural hub, for good or ill, the phenomenon bears our name.

Outwardly, Minnesota Nice is about being courteous, respectful, and polite—to anyone and everyone—helpful and welcoming to strangers. The broader social correlate to this is evident, among other ways, in the high degree of civic mindedness and social tolerance that's a central part of the culture here. It's also marked by a high degree of reserve; an aversion to confrontation and outward "unpleasantness"; a certain amount of self-deprecation, paired with a strong disinclination to stand out or appear different from the norm; a marked discomfort with strong displays of feeling or emotion. There's a running joke about the Swedish (or Norwegian or German) farmer who loved his wife so much, he almost told her.

But that sense of personal reserve that's such a big part of Minnesota Nice has a huge, largely hidden, dark side. This is, in part, because the wellsprings of this reserve come from the history of placing an extremely high value on a rather extreme version of self-sufficiency. When your neighbor is in trouble, you help him. When you're in trouble, your neighbor helps you. But when the crisis is over, the clear expectation is that you'll each immediately return to your intensely guarded, exceedingly private lives. Talk to anybody with deep roots in this region and you'll hear stories about neighbors going above and beyond the call to help neighbors recover from the devastation of the Big Tornado, the Big Flood. When disaster strikes, farmers and ranchers and even city people pitch in, sandbagging riverbanks, feeding and housing and praying with the displaced, searching for the missing, rebuilding splintered barns and homes.

And Minnesotans constantly extend that cultural commitment of aid and caring outward to circles far removed from their own. When Hurricane Katrina hit, Minnesotans were strongly represented in the throng of volunteers who lent their labor and logistical assistance to the people of Louisiana. Minnesota has a well-deserved reputation as a place where refugees from strife-torn nations are welcomed with open arms, not just Europeans, but large numbers of Africans and Asians as well. But when the immigrants have been helped to resettle and the "welcome wagon" is gone, it is well and truly gone. The unspoken expectation is that any further assistance or support should be unnecessary. To paraphrase a line from Bob Dylan's "Just Like Tom Thumb's Blues," *Because we don't need you, and man, we expect the same.*

I was talking about this phenomenon with a writing student of mine after class one night, a woman who had grown up on a farm in the Red River Valley. "Yup," she said, "our families always had each others' backs when it came to shared disasters—natural disasters and such. Because those things that just happen—a blizzard, a flood, maybe even a fire—those things aren't your fault. But God forbid you should still need some kind of help after the trouble'd blown over. And God help you if you had a problem that folks just seemed to feel was of your own making. Depression, some other kind of mental health issue, marriage problems, family issues between parents and kids—you name it. You'd be on your own. That kind of stuff was strictly your family's business. Extended family, too, I guess. *Blood* family. But nobody else's."

So, that's how it is with outsiders, too. When people come here in need of a safe place to make a fresh start, the culture of Minnesota Nice is glad to welcome them and help them make the transition to their new life on the prairie. But the unspoken rules that the newcomers are supposed to intuit include these: "Assimilate, and do it quickly; understand that, if you're still having problems after you've had a couple of years or so to settle in, then we're going to start seeing your very presence here as a problem."

Minnesota Not-Nice

There are many examples of anti-immigrant and racist violence in Minnesota's history, and it started at the beginning: For the white Americans who came to this area in the 1840s and '50s, the presence of the Dakota and Ojibwe people was a problem. The invaders made taking the land their highest priority, signing treaties they did not keep. The Dakota, at the edge of starvation, went to war in 1862, and thirty-eight Dakota men were hanged in the aftermath. An uneasy cold war over abrogated treaty rights has reigned ever since.

Yankees in Minneapolis hanged an effigy of St. Patrick in 1858, which incited a day of rioting among Irish immigrants.[1] One aspect of the struggle to achieve a place in the American "mainstream" has often been that as one group ascends the ladder toward this status, they stomp on the hands of the groups attempting to climb up just behind them. Irish dock workers in St. Paul demonstrated a prime example of this phenomenon when, in 1863, fearing competition for jobs, they threatened arriving "contrabands"—black families escaping slavery in Missouri—who had to disembark at Fort Snelling, instead.[2]

Lumber and mining barons fighting mounting labor unrest in Minnesota's northern Arrowhead and Iron Range area were deeply concerned over the immigration of Finnish socialists into the region. In 1910, they used new speculation from the world of anthropology and the new pseudoscience of eugenics regarding the origins of the Finnish people to launch a bizarre campaign in the courts to refuse naturalization of seventeen Finns on the grounds that they were Asian—"Mongolian"—and thus ineligible under the Chinese Exclusion Act. This would have stemmed the tide of Finnish immigration to America.[3]

In 1920, a trio of black circus workers was lynched in downtown Duluth.[4]

The Ku Klux Klan came to Minnesota in the 1920s, with hundreds of members in communities throughout the state, regular state conventions, picnics, and cross burnings; it declined by the end of the decade, after scandals in Indiana's Klan leadership were exposed.[5]

---

[1] "St. Patrick's Day in Minneapolis!" *St. Anthony Falls Evening News*, March 18, 1858, 2, www.kinsource.com/MinnesotaTales/totw2008/stpatricksday18mar1858.htm.

[2] William D. Green, *A Peculiar Imbalance: The Fall and Rise of Racial Equality in Early Minnesota* (St. Paul: Minnesota Historical Society Press, 2007), 130–37.

[3] Carl Ross, *The Finn Factor in American Labor, Culture and Society* (New York Mills, MN: Parta Publishers, 1977), 115.

[4] Michael Fedo, *The Lynchings in Duluth* (St. Paul: Borealis Books, 2000).

[5] Elizabeth Dorsey Hatle and Nancy M. Viallancourt, "Minnesota's Ku Klux Klan in the 1920s," *Minnesota History* (Winter 2009–10): 360–71, collections.mnhs.org/mnhistorymagazine/articles/61/v61i08p360-371.pdf.

In 1931, a black family, the Lees, were nearly driven from their South Minneapolis home by an angry white mob who wanted them out of the neighborhood.[6]

For the most part, though, discrimination in Minnesota hasn't been about lynching, or the burning of crosses on lawns, or overt, public acts of bigotry. The culture of Minnesota Nice has meant that the face of discrimination has almost always been much more subtle here. But the kind of subtlety that underlies Minnesota Nice—extreme and highly nuanced—only makes racism harder to fight. A subtlety this deep is denial's best friend—makes it too easy to slip into a state of constant denial and remain there. But whether crippling pain comes to you due to deliberate malice or as the unintended consequence of someone's thoughtless action or heedless inaction, the result feels much the same on the receiving end. When we hear a white person say, "Oh, but I don't even see color," the subtext we really hear tells us, loud and clear, that what they don't see is us: that our identity, our perspective, our whole *history* is insignificant, not worthy of attention.

Recent reports in both the national and the local press remind us that disparities between Minnesota's black and white populations of all kinds—in terms of income, health outcomes, educational outcomes, and more—rank persistently among the very worst reported by any state in the nation. How can this possibly be, in a state that, generally, ranks so high compared to other states on every major index of livability? How can a place renowned for its hospitality and its progressive values have proven to be so profoundly inhospitable toward its people of color?

Part of the reason has its roots in the fact that, up until recent years, the black population of the state has been so small compared to that of most other states. The big battlefields of the Reconstruction Era (in the immediate aftermath of the Civil War) and of the civil rights movement had all lain elsewhere, far

---

[6] Steve Brant, "Site of Racial Showdown in Minneapolis Heading to National Register," *Star Tribune* (Minneapolis), July 24, 2014.

away. From roughly 1915 to 1970, millions of African Americans left the South in search of a better life, migrating to cities north and west, but the massive social dislocation sparked by this Great Migration largely missed Minnesota.

Fair-minded and progressive Minnesotans were watching, though, and throughout the 1950s and the turbulent 1960s, pro–civil rights sentiment in Minnesota grew until it became very strong. But it's easy to take the moral high road on a social issue when your personal commitment to the principals you espouse remains largely untested. It's easy to point a finger at the egregious violation of basic human rights going on elsewhere in the country and ignore the widespread, if less obvious, violations going on in your own backyard.

Contemporary Minnesotans are often genuinely shocked to hear that there was active, ongoing slavery at Fort Snelling from the 1820s through the 1850s—and that as recently as the mid-1950s, black residents and visitors to Minnesota were refused service at restaurants and hotels, even in the downtown Twin Cities. Housing and job discrimination were as prevalent here as they were anywhere else in the country. White Minnesota is part and parcel of white America, after all, and is profoundly influenced by the same prejudice and bigotry that has been so omnipresent in the rest of the country. But up here in the cool blue North, there was no long, bitter history of blood on the soil between black and white, no multigenerational saga of mutual hatred and violence.

African American refugees from other places in America who *did* share this kind of wretched history often found Minnesota a breath of fresh air, a place where a family could manage—through hard work, persistence, and a healthy dose of good luck—to build a life relatively free of overt hatred and less hindered by the barriers to black progress erected by Jim Crow. The numbers of black people who eventually ventured up this way to join them grew to a steady trickle throughout the 1960s and 1970s, lured, in part, by a social/political climate that was friendly toward racial justice, strongly influenced by the activist careers of people like Hubert Humphrey, Roy Wilkins, Nellie Stone Johnson, Harry Davis,

Josie Johnson, and others. The leadership at many of Minnesota's corporate giants like 3M, General Mills, Cargill, and Pillsbury laid out a welcome mat, signing on early to help address the persistent issue of unequal access to quality employment by aggressively seeking African American managers and workers willing to relocate here. The black workers who arrived to claim these positions possessed the training and the education to take the opportunity and run with it. The state's civic boosters, politicians, and corporate giants who had garnered lots of positive attention for this took the opportunity that came with all the accolades to pat themselves on the back.

Things were looking pretty good in the Land of Good Intentions. The boosters helped create, for a minute, a powerful national buzz about the Good Life up in Minnesota.

But things were quite different for the larger waves of black immigrants who turned up here in search of that good life throughout the 1980s, the 1990s, and the early years of the new century. They came in search of jobs, not to claim jobs that were already promised and waiting for them, and they came, many of them, without much education, specialized job skills, or training. They came, desperate to find a safer place to raise their children, a place where you could let your kids out to play without worrying about stray bullets, a place where your family could rest easy at night, their dreams undisturbed by the steady *pop, pop, pop* of random gunfire from dusk 'til dawn.

They came in large numbers. The state's black and African American population grew from 53,342 in 1980 to 274,412 in 2010 (plus another 36,912 biracial people who identified themselves as "white plus black or African American"). And some of the problems they had fled Chicago or Detroit or Cleveland or East St. Louis to escape came with them . . . which made many long-established Minnesotans, at best, very uneasy with the new immigrants. On the other end of the spectrum, some Minnesotans were outraged, angry, and fearful. Public alarms were raised about people who supposedly came because they heard that you could show up in Minnesota and claim a bigger, easier welfare check.

The truth is that in the entire history of the social safety net, it's highly improbable that anybody has *ever* uprooted their family and moved them five hundred miles from home in order to collect an "easy" welfare check—because by conscious design, no part of the system is "easy," not even in Minnesota. The only people who say it is are the people who've never had to navigate it.

At least there *is* a safety net . . . but through a close observation of its workings, it's easy to discern and "decode" how the country really feels about the people who find themselves having to rely on that safety net to survive. *Unintelligent*—if they were smarter, they would surely have found other means to avoid the difficulty they're in; *lazy/unmotivated*—there's ample work around for anybody who *wants* to work, if you'll just show some initiative and look. The real problem with such hardened attitudes—of all kinds—is that they're often clandestine . . . hidden. Asked directly if they hold such beliefs, many people will sincerely deny that they do. Some people are genuinely *unaware* that they do.

But this phenomenon of the hidden power of subterranean belief has always had the chilling effect of making some such beliefs more powerful than the beliefs that people openly proclaim. This often results in public policy that is at odds with the ideals that people say they believe in. And it dovetails in a dangerous way with the worst manifestations of Minnesota Nice: warm and welcoming on the outside; cold and indifferent on the inside.

Anyone who has ever been in a difficult, complicated relationship knows that the opposite of love is not hate. It's indifference. Neglect is indifference's twin sister. And there is no such thing as benign neglect. Neglect is, in its truest meaning, a verb. And like twin horsemen of the apocalypse, Neglect and Indifference have teamed up to cause a lot of damage.

The evidence of the damage is everywhere to be seen: failing schools; high concentrations of persistent poverty in failing neighborhoods; the egregious over-incarceration of people of color; an alarming number of annual incidents in which people of color are shot by the police or end up dead in police custody. How did things get so bad, even here?

History Matters

As always, it helps to know the history. Minnesota's soldiers returned from the Civil War thinking, "Union restored; slavery finished; problem fixed." The slaves had been freed. Why wasn't their community exploding with vigor, enthusiasm, and industry, looking to make the most of their newfound liberty? Why were they still having problems? "Why, after all this time, aren't they becoming more like us?"

Any reader of the fledgling black press during Reconstruction would be mightily impressed at the astonishing degree to which the recently freed slaves were, indeed, deeply grateful . . . were, indeed, working with great vigor, enthusiasm, and industry to build a better life for themselves and their community. But even though two hundred thousand black soldiers had just served bravely and nobly in the cause of Union, they found themselves still excluded from every new opportunity. The promised forty acres and a mule were never delivered. White veterans in the tens of thousands got an opportunity to help this nation-building effort in the underpopulated West—in places like Kansas, Nebraska, and Oklahoma—along with an opportunity to build a personal legacy of prosperity that they could hand down to future generations. Black veterans got . . . lectures about "bootstraps" and hard work—something about which they already knew plenty. There would be no help forthcoming, no assistance in lifting themselves out of abject poverty and the shadow-world of life on the extreme margins as second-class citizens. Instead, there were Black Codes (spelling out where black people could go and could not go; requiring annual and unbreakable labor contracts; demanding fees from any who worked in any occupation besides farmer and servant) and Jim Crow domestic terrorism. Now that slavery was gone, what black people encountered was the cold reality that the rest of America still seems so completely unready to admit: that *America's real original sin was not slavery, but white supremacy.* The law may say Jim Crow is dead . . . but if it is, then it's having a long and vigorous afterlife.

I was doing some neighborhood organizing work in Chicago during the summer of 1970. When I told a friend there that I was getting ready to come live in Minneapolis for awhile, he said, "Aw, brother, really? Why? Worst cops in the whole world up there, man!"

I used to volunteer at a residential substance abuse program in South Minneapolis. After finishing my last tutoring session one evening, I started walking home about 7:30 PM. Just as I crossed the street, a car came tearing up at high speed, and three plainclothes police officers leaped out with guns in hand. They identified themselves, and then one of them holstered his gun, threw me up against the trunk of the car, and cuffed me.

I asked why. One of the officers pulled a handgun from his boot—a personal, non-regulation weapon—held it against my head, removed the safety, and cocked it. That's a helluva sound—a gun being cocked while jammed tightly against the dome of your skull. Intimidating. I *was* intimidated. But more than anything, I was angry. And it occurred to me, even in the heat of the moment, that this was exactly the reaction he wanted . . . like someone who lights a fire and thinks, *Now, let me throw a little gasoline on there.* Instead of answering my question, the cowboy with the gun to my head told me not to move, then shoved my head hard to one side with the barrel and said, "Wouldn't even breathe real hard if I was you. This gun's got a hair trigger." There was another reason to be wary of that gun. I knew countless stories of weapons like that, produced from a boot or the small of an officer's back, meant to be placed in a suspect's hand or close to his body should he somehow end up dead by the time the encounter was over.

One of the other officers finally spoke up: "Liquor store was robbed a couple blocks away about twenty minutes ago by somebody who matches your description." As they inspected my ID and the other contents of my wallet, I told him as calmly as I could that right across the street, there was a whole building full of people who could vouch for who I was and where I'd been all evening. All three cops heard this, but they ignored it. It was as if I hadn't said anything at all.

They threw me into the back of their car and radioed that they'd arrested a suspect. As they began to pull away from the curb, a voice on their radio told them to stay put. A lieutenant pulled up in a plain car behind us and talked with the officers while I listened to the police chatter coming over the airwaves.

The suspect was described as a light-skinned black male, about five foot seven, with extremely close-cropped hair and a slight mustache, wearing a knee-length, light tan leather coat. That was the only time I gave them attitude. I smirked a little and asked them, "That supposed to be *me?*" I stood about five foot ten in my boots, and I'm a medium brown . . . not someone that anybody has ever described as "light-skinned." I wear glasses and was then sporting a scraggly goatee. And at that time, I had what might have been the biggest, baddest Afro in the entire state of Minnesota—a foot-tall brain-cloud kind of Afro, as far from "close-cropped" as it's possible for hair to get. And I was wearing a waist-length, almost sepia leather coat, nothing remotely like the one in the description.

The lieutenant heard this, too. He flashed his badge at me and said to them, "Guys . . . *really?* Cut this guy loose." Just like that. One of them spit, a couple of them grumbled, they uncuffed me and pulled me back out of their car, returned my wallet, and then tore off back down the street. No, "Oh, well, sorry, sir," from them. Nothing.

I knew, as I tried to shake it off while walking home, that other scenes like this were playing out that evening in any number of other places in America. What if that non-regulation gun the cowboy cop had pressed against my head really *did* have a hair trigger? If I had reacted angrily and resisted, I might well have been killed, as have so many others before me and since, in just such an encounter.

There's a history to encounters like these. And if you understand this history, even a little, you understand that all the hue and cry about "weeding a few bad apples" out of police departments and doing some retraining will not fix our problem. It is important to weed "bad apples" like that cowboy out of our police departments. But the core of the problem is that although undeniable racial progress has been made, the large numbers of African Americans left behind in intractable poverty are still stuck in the same cultural space as our ancestors were when just newly freed from slavery: stuck on the margins as perpetual outsiders in the land of their birth; feared; stigmatized as criminal by nature. This mostly subterranean attitude applies, in general, to other low-income communities of color as well.

So, the hard truth is that police departments deal with communities of color in exactly the way that American society, Minnesota society, has asked them to. There's a readily observable pattern: people who find themselves routinely locked out of equal opportunity will generally find themselves locked up to roughly that same degree. Racially based restrictive housing covenants were declared unconstitutional in 1948, but they have continued in practice. Until 1972, thousands of municipalities had vagrancy laws on the books that were about regulating black people's lives. Even though those laws have long since been struck down, the racist beliefs that created and sustained them are still very much around—and as a consequence, too many police officers sometimes behave as though they're still on the books. The result is that simply being young and black or brown is a de facto "status crime." It's not necessary to *do* anything wrong . . . just step outside on the street or get behind the wheel of your car, and you could already be in trouble.

Listen

As many black families pulled up stakes and left the communities where they'd been born and raised, searching for a better life, this part of the collective African American story never seemed to be grasped by the communities to which they moved, Minnesota included. Truly welcoming weary strangers into your company means, first, learning something about their story. How else can you possibly begin to divine what assistance or support they might need from you as they begin to build a new life? But

Minnesotans, like other Americans, have seldom known or, seemingly, haven't *cared* to know much about the stories of the non-European populations with whom they share this land.

Minnesotans evince little knowledge of the history of settler aggression or the widespread and egregious abrogation of treaty rights when it comes to the experiences of indigenous peoples native to this soil. There is precious little understanding of the diverse histories of our Chicano/Latino populations, many of whom long ago became citizens, not because they crossed international borders to get here, but because the U.S. border *crossed over them* as a result of the massive amount of land seized from Mexico at the end of the Mexican War. A story that can be told in easily graspable, shorthand form (think Hmong refugees whose men had helped the U.S. war effort in Southeast Asia, forced to flee their old homeland to escape reprisals) stirs sympathy enough to mobilize an organized resettlement effort. But even that only goes so far. There is little patience here for immigrants from anywhere—Asian and Pacific Islander, African, Latino—or even Americans from much closer to home, like Chicago, who seem slow to assimilate. Ojibwe and Dakota people get the same treatment. And there's a stark, simple equation at work here: if you fail to value a people's stories, you fail to value *them*.

In sharp contrast to this, new immigrants are always listening for and trying to make sense of the stories of their adopted land. But here in the North Country, immigrants scramble to figure out for themselves the many unspoken rules about how to live in harmony with Minnesota Nice. And some of these rules are damned hard. They learn that no matter how angry and aggrieved you may feel, given the history of what's happened to you and your people, you're still expected to abide by the unspoken mandate to "kwitchurbeliakin." That's "Quit Your Belly Achin'," for the uninitiated. Because life is just not fair. Period. So, whatever's happened to you, suck it up and move on. It's not okay to outwardly show anger or resentment in any way. This is evidence of weakness. And it's not *nice*.

Being a true Minnesotan also means being self-sufficient. All cultures express this value in some way, but Minnesota's is the most extreme iteration I've ever encountered. My introduction to at least one man's version of this ideal came from a mechanic named Bud. He owned and ran a car-repair shop in a South Minneapolis neighborhood that, over decades, he'd seen transition from mostly white, mixed middle and working class, to largely working class and poor people of color.

In an area that had become about 60 percent black, and whose population had been steadily getting younger, the only customers ever seen coming or going were white men over forty. In inner-city neighborhoods of color, places like that become unofficially recognized as "no go zones." Doesn't look like your business is welcome there, so . . . you simply erase them from your mental map of the neighborhood, to the extent that when you pass by, you literally don't even see them anymore. But on the day Bud and I met, the family car was giving me big trouble and I happened to be just a block or two from his place, so I figured it was a good day to stop in and take my chances.

Word was that the guy was racist, but after a little conversation, it didn't feel that way to me. The more we talked, the more it occurred to me that, really, Bud was just generally a grumpy old bastard . . . and that he probably tended to instantly distrust and dismiss anybody who found it hard to deal with this fact. As I look back on our encounter from the perspective of someone who's become a grumpy old bastard himself, I'm even more convinced of this.

I told him what the car was doing, but he cut me off, grunting his diagnosis before I could even finish. "Alternator. Ain't got time for that today . . . but I got one I could sell ya." When I told him that I'd never replaced one and wouldn't know where to begin—told him I'd just go on and walk home if he thought he'd have time to fix it for me the next day—he shot me a searing look of pity mixed with disgust and said, simply, *A man ought never pay another man to do something he could do for himself.*

This pronouncement felt stunningly sharp and severe, especially coming from the mouth of someone who did, after all, make his living from doing the repairs that his customers didn't care to do. His words made me wonder what he must think of most of us men walking around his rapidly changing neighborhood, black and brown men, none of whom had come up, as he did, on a hardscrabble farm established by Norwegian immigrant grandparents who made the clothes they wore and who ate, almost entirely, only the food they grew themselves. People for whom life was hard . . . but who never complained. I thought about us black men from the neighborhood who walk around looking sullen and sad, and how men like Bud must look at us and wonder why. They don't *see* much, if any, evidence of the discrimination that keeps us angry and on edge. They certainly don't see how they've ever *personally* been guilty of committing an act of discrimination against us or anyone else. We don't "get" each other. They don't tend to understand much about how the world looks to us, and we don't tend to understand much about how the world looks to them. So, even though some of the time we share the same space, we avoid talking . . . and when we must, we keep it superficial, allowing ourselves to come tantalizingly close for an instant, but then spiraling past each other like separate galaxies, each on its own axis, into the void.

As Bud's words sank in, I turned to leave, but then suddenly, something in me wouldn't *let* me leave on that note. I felt the need to challenge him, surprise him, through a small, spontaneous gesture, aimed at bridging that yawning, silent gulf between us, if only for a moment. "Okay, then," I said. "Wanna take a minute or two and show me how to do it myself?" Without needing even a moment to think about it, he surprised *me* by pulling out the tools I'd need and agreeably talking me through the job while he sipped strong coffee and went back to working on the car he'd been fixing when I walked in.

As we worked side by side in his tiny shop, I eased into a story about my own people—how generations of my folk struggled, always managing to creatively "make a way from no way." He didn't say much. But he was listening. My attempt to paint as vivid a picture for him as I could of the people I come from—people who also took what life threw their way and didn't complain—seemed to resonate with him. Mid-job, I noticed there was a sign on the wall stating that it was illegal for customers to be back there in the shop, an edict he'd apparently decided to ignore in my case. Even though he stepped in to help me replace and tighten the belts, he also decided to completely ignore the sign that said, "Shop Charge, $45 hr.," because when I pulled out my checkbook to pay for the parts and asked why I shouldn't pay him at least enough to split the difference on time with him, he said, "Well . . . why? Done it yourself, din't ya?"

Minnesota Nice can be *really* nice. Interesting and complicated too.

Bridging the gulf between us is *hard*. It takes courage and effort. And the effort often results in an encounter that can be both unrewarding and unpleasant. But what alternative do we have? The demographic makeup of Minnesota, like the rest of the country, is changing rapidly and radically. By 2050, the majority of America's citizens will be comprised of groups who used to be called "minorities." The majority here in Minnesota is likely to remain white for some time, but populations of color, especially the Latino population, will see a dramatic increase. The Somali population of the state was already so large by the year 2000 that Islam quietly supplanted Judaism as the state's second most prominent religious faith.

As we move forward, we can lean on this: that although it tends to happen slowly and only with great, conscious effort, people and cultures *do* change in response to the changing realities and needs of their times. If we are to sort ourselves out and make good lives for ourselves in this ever-more-multicultural landscape, we've got to start by talking less and listening more. We can listen—really listen—to one another's stories and learn from them. Collectively, we can learn to tell a story that includes *all* our stories . . . fashion a mosaic-like group portrait from those stories that we all can agree truly does resemble *people like us*.

SEEDS FOR SEVEN GENERATIONS

Diane Wilson

Diane Wilson (Dakota) has published a memoir, *Spirit Car: Journey to a Dakota Past*, the 2012 One Minneapolis One Read selection, and a nonfiction book, *Beloved Child: A Dakota Way of Life*. Wilson is a 2013 Bush Foundation Fellow and executive director for Dream of Wild Health, a nonprofit farm.

We cared for our corn in those days as we would care for a child; for we Indian people loved our gardens, just as a mother loves her children; and we thought that our growing corn liked to hear us sing, just as children like to hear their mother sing to them. . . . The singing was begun in the spring and continued until the corn was ripe.

—Buffalo Bird Woman, *Buffalo Bird Woman's Garden*

On a warm afternoon in mid-June, a small group of children moved slowly down the path between two long, raised garden beds. A few of the children were as young as eight years old; all of them were from Native families living in the Twin Cities. They were Ojibwe, Dakota, Lakota, HoChunk, Oneida, and Diné. Most of them had never gardened before, never held a corn seed in their small, damp hands. One young girl did not know that food bought at the store came from the vegetables harvested daily from the soil.

But on this summer afternoon, they were quiet in their anticipation of planting a Dakota corn seed that has rarely been grown, much less eaten, in the many years since the Dakota were removed from Minnesota after the 1862 U.S.–Dakota War. They had already learned from an Arapaho elder, Ernie Whiteman, that the garden was on Dakota homeland, land that has not known these seeds for many generations. Now they listened closely as Ernie showed them how to plant six seeds in each mounded hill and pat the earth firmly over each seed.

While the children planted, elder Hope Flanagan sang a traditional song in her clear, strong voice. As always, the music woke something in us, elevating the simple act of planting seeds to a connection with the sacred, a moment of remembering what it means to be Native. Even the birds seemed to listen, circling overhead as they drew closer to the fields.

In the quiet that followed Hope's song, one of the youngest girls said, this is how we used to dance for our corn. She slowly moved each foot in an intuitive dance that reconnected the spirits of these children with their ancestors. As she danced to the blood memory of an ancient tradition, the hearts of the adults— all of whom carry the scars of historical trauma—were uplifted. Estella LaPointe, a beautiful Lakota woman, would later say that helping children plant this corn was healing for her.

As I watched, I thought of my mother, who was enrolled at the Rosebud Reservation and grew up in a boarding school on the Pine Ridge Reservation. After her family fled the Depression in South Dakota to look for work in Minneapolis, she married a young man of Swedish descent and raised her children far removed from any Native community. My siblings and I attended predominantly white schools where we learned a version of history that could not explain my mother's silence about her past, why she and my aunts attended boarding schools, or why she received an annual check for allotment land in South Dakota that was so small she and my aunts used to laugh about their inheritance. My father, on the other hand, recognized only that we were white, like him.

As an adult, I spent many years learning who my mother's family was, a process that forced me to discover a different history from the one I was taught in school. Our family story led me to the dark truth about the genocide of Native people in this country and the earlier generations of children who were forced to attend boarding schools. My family's small role in this history had been shaped by government policies that ultimately threatened either assimilation or extermination. Finally, I understood my mother's silence. I was left with the question of what, if anything, I could do to transform the legacy of pain and loss that I had inherited.

This long journey brought me here, to this field, to these seeds. When a friend told me about Dream of Wild Health, a small garden where they were growing out old seeds that had come from tribes around the region, I immediately asked if I could volunteer. This was, perhaps, my own blood memory rising up, a call to remember a relationship with the earth, with plants and animals, that dates back to our earliest ancestors. The seeds hold that memory; they can help us recover who we are as Native people through the simple act of growing our own food once again. With each seed that we plant, we are reclaiming one of our richest cultural legacies: our traditional foods.

As it was with my family, I had to learn the story, or history, that could explain the heartbreaking rift between Native people and the land. Only then could I understand what Ernie once told us: "If you control the food, you can control the people." By reconnecting with our own stories, we know what was taken away, and the lessons we need to teach our children.

Long ago corn was a gift to the Dakota at a time when the medicine people were concerned about a shortage of food. They had heard that a Being living at the bottom of a lake could help the people survive. A young girl bravely swam toward the bottom where a woman dressed in white buckskin gave her a gift: four male corn seeds in one bowl and four female corn seeds in another. The Sacred Woman explained how to plant the seeds so that the Dakota people would always have plenty of food.

Afterward, they gave thanks to the Creator and held their first green corn dance. They named this lake Spirit Lake for the holy being who gave them the gift of corn.

Corn became one of the foods that the Dakota relied on as part of their seasonal food cycles. In June, the month when the strawberries were ripe, corn was planted on ground where there was a good growth of wild artichokes, indicating rich soil. While some corn was dried and saved as seed or as food in bark containers for the winter, women generally grew only enough corn to eat for a few weeks. In September, families moved to the lakes for harvesting wild rice, which once grew all around the Twin Cities area. When Louis Hennepin visited the Dakota living near Mille Lacs in 1680, he was fed wild rice seasoned with dried blueberries and smoked fish eggs, served on a bark platter.

Throughout the summer, women gathered wild foods, including berries, plums, nuts, *psincha* and *psinchincha*, roots growing at the bottom of shallow lakes that women harvested by feeling for them with their feet. They dug wild turnips or *tipsin* using sharp sticks, water-lily root, and the *mdo*, a potato-like root. In November, the deer-rutting moon, the Dakota hunted deer, followed by ice fishing in January and muskrat hunting in March, which was also maple sugar time. Throughout the year, food gathering activities were honored with prayers, songs, and ceremonies.

The Dakota also hunted bison, elk, and deer living in the tallgrass prairie, an immense area that included southern and western Minnesota. Described as a sea of grass, the prairie was formed over thousands of years through a fortuitous combination of glacial till, wind-dropped organic material, manure from grazing animals, aeration by prairie dogs, and an occasional fire. The result was a vast landscape with deep topsoil and hundreds of species of plants and animals. Yet none of them were as important to the physical and spiritual health of the Dakota as the bison. Lakota medicine man John Fire Lame Deer once said:

> The buffalo gave us everything we needed. Without it we were nothing. Our tipis were made of his skin. His hide

was our bed, our blanket, our winter coat. It was our
drum, throbbing through the night, alive, holy. Out of
his skin we made our water bags. His flesh strengthened
us, became flesh of our flesh. Not the smallest part of it
was wasted. His stomach, a red-hot stone dropped into
it, became our soup kettle. His horns were our spoons,
the bones our knives, our women's awls and needles. Out
of his sinews we made our bowstrings and thread. His
ribs were fashioned into sleds for our children, his hoofs
became rattles. His mighty skull, with the pipe leaning
against it, was our sacred altar.

This spiritually based and ingenious use of every aspect of an
animal or plant demonstrated deep gratitude and respect com-
bined with a sophisticated understanding of the natural world.
As Jack Weatherford tells us in his book *Indian Givers*, in the
time before Columbus, indigenous tribes of the Americas developed three-fifths of the world's crops, including corn, potatoes,
squash, and beans, gifts that today are seldom acknowledged.
Traditional diets were based on locally grown, seasonal, whole
foods, with no evidence of "lifestyle" diseases such as type 2 diabetes that are such overwhelming issues today. Over centuries
of close relationship with the Plant Nation, Native people accumulated a vast knowledge of plant properties that became the
basis for modern pharmacology. They also knew they needed to
maintain balance and harmony between hunters, gatherers, and
the environment in which they lived in a way that ensured their
long-term survival.

In Dakota we say, Mitakuye Oyasin, which means "all my relations." We understand that all beings have a spirit and we are
required, as good relatives, to treat all of our relations—including
plants, animals, air, water, land—with respect. As Ella Deloria
explained in *Speaking of Indians*, "The ultimate aim of Dakota life,
stripped of accessories, was quite simple: One must obey kinship rules; one must be a good relative." Acting as a good relative
meant accepting many rules and responsibilities, from a sense of

restraint in harvesting only what was needed to offering hospitality and food to every visitor. Ella described the elders as saying, "Give food! Give food unstintingly! Let nothing be held in reserve for one alone. When all food is gone, then we shall honorably starve together. Let us still be Dakotas!"

When the Europeans arrived bearing iron kettles and hoes, guns, beads, and cloth, these gifts were welcomed as useful new tools. Native women married fur traders, creating kinship responsibilities as well as economic opportunities for both sides. In the early years these relationships were managed by assimilating traders into the tribe.

By the nineteenth century, however, an insatiable desire for land brought immense pressure and new changes to both the Dakota and the Minnesota landscape. Between 1830 and 1900, virtually all of the tallgrass prairie was plowed under by European settlers eager to establish homesteads and farms on this virgin, fertile soil. As this rich habitat was diminished, plants disappeared and the bison moved further west, greatly reducing the availability of traditional foods for the Dakota. The largest, most diverse ecosystem in the central United States was virtually destroyed within seventy years.

In its place came a new form of agriculture: monoculture. Early farmers began to shift from basic subsistence farming that included a variety of crops and livestock to growing vast fields of wheat as a cash crop. By 1890 Minnesota was the national leader in wheat production, aided by new developments in farm technology.

Surrendering to immense pressure to relinquish much of their land in the treaties of 1851 and 1857, the Dakota were placed on a small reservation alongside the Minnesota River where they struggled to survive on government-issued commodity goods and annuity payments. In 1862, families neared starvation while the agent refused to make treaty payments from a warehouse filled with food that belonged to them, and the tensions between the Dakota and settlers exploded in a six-week war. Afterward, treaties were abrogated and all reservation lands seized as the

Dakota were forcibly removed from the state to a harsh, make-shift reservation in Crow Creek, South Dakota. In the first few years, the Dakota and HoChunk—who were also removed de-spite not participating in the war—lost an estimated six hundred children to starvation and disease.

As Minnesota was building its reputation as the primary wheat producer in the nation, in 1878 the first federal boarding school was opened in Carlisle, Pennsylvania. With the support of both the federal government and churches, nearly five hundred new schools were created for the purpose of assimilating Native children by forbidding their languages and spirituality and forc-ing them to dress and act according to European values. Typically underfunded, the schools provided inadequate diets, and thou-sands of children suffered from malnutrition, disease, and even death.

By the 1930s and 1940s, many tribes had been relocated to reservations, essentially surrendering their traditional foods and medicines as they were forced to surrender their homelands. The vast knowledge of the natural world that had been accumulated over many generations was displaced as families turned to the federal government's commodity food program to survive. Tra-ditional diets were replaced with high-starch, high-fat foods that further undermined the health of Native people, leading to esca-lating levels of diabetes and heart disease.

Despite pressure from the government, tribes were slow to adapt to the demand that they, too, begin to cultivate the land using European methods, a system that violated indigenous val-ues of respect and reciprocity for all beings, including plants and animals. The clash between cultures that began in 1492 was as much about our drastically different food systems as it was about our differing values, languages, and spirituality. Throughout the government's multifaceted assimilation policies, controlling Na-tive food systems has been a consistent, and deadly, theme.

By the turn of the twentieth century, decades of growing wheat as a monoculture crop had exhausted Minnesota's rich soil. Farmers diversified into horticulture, sheep, corn, and dairy production and began to rotate crops to help sustain the health of the soil. After World War II, farmers focused on corn and soybean production, a shift that ultimately led to our current industrialized farm system of growing limited crops using intensive chemical fertilizers and pesticides and relying on genetically modified seeds. As recently as 150 years ago, the United States did not have a commercial seed industry. Today, companies like Monsanto control what has become the world's largest commercial seed industry, promoting a form of genetic Manifest Destiny throughout the world.

This modern-day agricultural system represents a profound cultural shift toward treating the earth, and the foods she provides, as commodities. If the land is a commodity, she can be sold; if our plants and animals are commodities, they can be grown in factories under conditions that emphasize profits rather than relationships. If our children are targeted as consumers, they can be manipulated to depend on foods that will shorten their life expectancy. Our children will be the first generation to live shorter lives than we will. How our communities eat and how our food is grown is intimately connected to the environmental issues we face. The food choices we make create the world we live in.

Despite the claims that an industrialized food system is needed in order to feed our rapidly expanding global population, in Minnesota, hunger has doubled over the past five years. Children account for 40 percent of Minnesota's hungry. A sixth of the world's population is now hungry, while diet-related diseases in this country are reaching epidemic levels that disproportionately affect low-income communities of color.

When the challenges we face seem overwhelming, I remember the words of Clifford Canku, a Dakota elder and spiritual leader from Sisseton. After a long conversation about historical trauma, he asked me to remind people that the past five hundred years is a short time in the history of Native people in this country. The Dakota have been present in this place, Mni Sota Makoce, for thousands of years, and it is our spirituality that has allowed us to survive. Tell them, he said, that's who Dakota people are, not the statistics you read in the paper. We are people who raise beloved children, who treat the earth as our mother, and who regard being a good relative to be of utmost importance to the community. Tell them that our ancestors suffered so that we could be happy.

Once we see that the past five hundred years is a break in our connection to this rich cultural legacy, then the question becomes how we begin to reclaim it. A Dakota elder, Glenn Wasicuna, explained that we do this healing work by returning to the traditional values that every tribe carries. In this way, we become the people that our ancestors were; we honor the sacrifices they made and the suffering they experienced.

We also do this healing work by returning to the traditional foods and medicines cherished by our ancestors and by relearning what it means to have a deep, loving relationship with the earth. For some of us, that means remembering that gardening is ceremony, as Dakota scholar and gardener Teresa Peterson has said, and reconnecting with the old seeds that were once planted and saved by generations of Native families. For many years, these seeds have been hidden away in drawers and jars, waiting to be grown once again as food for the people.

In 2000, Potawatomi elder and seed keeper Cora Baker wrote a letter to Dream of Wild Health—at that time a garden in Farmington—expressing her dying wish that Native people might once again begin to garden. She included her lifetime collection of seeds, many of them gifts from people passing by her garden: Mandan corn from North Dakota, Hopi black turtle beans, Lakota squash. A few came with stories of sorrow, like the Cherokee Trail of Tears corn. Others, like the traditional tobacco thought to be eight hundred years old, inspired awe. Without exception, these seeds had survived because they were nurtured by the people; and the people survived because they nurtured the seeds.

When I first heard about Cora's gift, something in my heart

immediately responded. As a gardener, I understood that her seeds were a fragile living record of the past, a tangible inheritance from our ancestors who knew that future generations, our generation, would need them for food. Our ancestors protected these seeds at all cost, knowing that they, like our children, are the future.

We began growing out Cora's seeds, a few varieties each season. In the beginning it was enough to simply help plant and grow any variety, regardless of its origin. And yet, as a Dakota woman and grandmother, I felt the lack of any Dakota corn in Cora Baker's gift, and I did not know of any Dakota corn being grown near the Twin Cities. Instead, we were surrounded by a vast sea of commercial, GMO corn.

In 2013, a gift of two varieties of Dakota corn from Teresa Peterson and the Science Museum of Minnesota allowed us the rich, healing experience of growing this corn on her homeland. Dakota families at Upper and Lower Sioux have protected these seeds by growing them in their own gardens and sharing them with other families. At Dream of Wild Health, this corn has now been planted by children of many different tribes. We are learning to work together across tribal borders as we reclaim one of the most important aspects of indigenous culture: our food. If today we plant Dakota corn, then tomorrow we plant seeds from other tribes, thereby ensuring the survival of all our precious foods.

Through my work at Dream of Wild Health, I have found a way to transform my family's experience into a renewed relationship with our community, the land, and these seeds. When seeds are planted with prayers and songs, tended with love, harvested with care, and shared with our community, then our food once again becomes the core of our culture. When we know where our food comes from, we can choose not to be victimized by an industrialized food system. Slowly, over many seasons, I have learned how the world view that rationalized the genocide of Native people is threatening the health and well-being of the earth, our food, and every living being.

As we plant the Dakota corn with children who are learning

about their traditional foods, we are rebuilding an indigenous relationship with the land. We are recognizing that one of the casualties in this long siege of assimilation has been our relationship with the earth that emphasized how we are all bound together in a web of relationships right down to the smallest bacteria. Many of us have forgotten that learning about plants and animals was a lifelong commitment, where the real test of living was to establish a balanced and harmonious relationship with nature. Why? Because our survival depends upon it.

Today many of our children are growing up in paved cities, afraid of bees, unable to recognize plants, and often completely ignorant of where their food comes from. And yet they will inherit this world; they will become its stewards. We are responsible for teaching our children that plants and animals are co-creating this world with us, and the lessons they offer can help us reverse the harms that humans have inflicted. As we say in Dakota, Mitakuye Oyasin. We Are All Related.

When we care for our Mother, when we raise healthy children, when we garden, returning to these old ways will help us transcend the trauma of the past, as well as that of the present, and provide healing for our ancestors. When the blood memory of our children remembers the green corn dance, that is the rhythm of the heart calling us home.

Sun Yung Shin is the author of a book of poetry/essays (*Unbearable Splendor*), two books of poetry (*Rough, and Savage* and *Skirt Full of Black,* and a children's book (*Cooper's Lesson*). She is also a co-editor of *Outsiders Within: Writing on Transracial Adoption.*